HOT DOGS SAVED MY LIFE!

Your Guide to Hot Dog Vending

By Ben Wilson
The Hot Dog Professor

Dedication

I wish to dedicate this book to all hot dog vendors and, even you, the potential vendor. I know the hot dog vending business can satisfy your income needs in the worst and best of times. My goal is to provide the most comprehensive guidance to help you get started, or to help you as you grow your current business.

I thank my wife, Sabrina, for her encouragement and support, and to Keith, who has been the best friend one could ask for. I thank L.A. O'Neil, who worked diligently to edit and manage this project, which never would have been completed without her guidance.

- The Hot Dog Professor

From Ben . . .

A Table of Contents allows one to jump to sections they deem important, while avoiding the task of skimming and scanning over the entire document, thus potentially missing crucial information. Everyone wants to get to the climax of a book, and I understand. But this book is one big climax! If you are serious about learning this business and you desire success – then read the entire book. Fold pages, take notes, use sticky notes and create your own tabs so that you can look back for reference from time to time. I promise that you will gain much more than the person who simply wants to learn only by skimming all of the information I'm providing in this book.

You've invested your hard-earned dollars to get this information; now let's get it inside that big brain of yours. By the way, I love that shirt! It really makes your eyes pop!

I wrote this all for you, not anyone else, and I will be here to help as you get going.

I can see you're a little miffed that I really don't have a table of contents.

So for you . . . just for you:

Table of Contents

I love you and wish you much success!

INTRODUCTION

After helping thousands of people get started in this business, hosting webinars, fighting for vendor rights, creating and publishing videos, building hot dog carts and, believe it or not, even running carts from time to time, I have decided to create a complete hot dog course. My goal is to give you, the hopeful vendor wannabe, all the tools, tips, tricks, warnings and advice that I have accumulated.

Experience is the mother of ~~invention~~ knowledge but, with three years of vending, I thankfully admit that not all of my knowledge is from experience. Fortunately, I have had the benefit of some of the most experienced hot dog vendors on the planet. Coupled with my own experience, my efforts and contact with hundreds of other vendors make the perfect recipe for success. Your success!

Yes, I want you to succeed. I want you to call, write, email or text me with your stories and questions. This is why I do it, and it's why I'm writing to you now.

I have included everything here, so don't hesitate to pull out the highlighter, maybe a pen or pencil, and take notes or even doodle on the pages. I won't get upset. This course should be used and abused; so, learn as much as you can, and then keep it handy as your business gets up and running.

Well, that's it, that's my fancy introduction.

Are you ready? No really, are you ready?

OK, then! Turn the page already!

This page was _not_ intentionally left blank. If it is, please feel free to grab that pen and highlighter you're supposed to have ready and give them a spin.

First:
Take the pen and write: "Ben is so smart."

Second: Take the highlighter and highlight: "Ben" and "smart."

Third: Smack your gullible self – this page ain't blank!

Chapter 22

The final chapter

Why in the world, would I put the last chapter of this course right here at the front? Easy. The final chapter of any book is usually the best, and I want us to start on the right foot. So, I'm putting my best foot – er – chapter forward.

How much can I really make? Are others really making it big? What makes this such a great business? Can I really do this? Others make this sound so easy, is it? You're probably just real lucky and I'm not.

Hold on! Wait a minute! Calm down! You have your pen/highlighter . . . maybe you need a drink, too! I'll answer all of your questions, so sit back and relax. I'm just getting started.

By the way, instead of typing out 'hot dog vendor' or 'vending' all the time, I will use an acronym. A *secret* acronym to prevent carpal tunnel for me, and carpal eyeball for you. The secret acronym is "HDV." OK. Got it? Good.

The HDV business can be a lifesaver; it can be what brings you from the brink of financial disaster or from financial ruin to success, giving you independence and propelling you to bigger and better things. Similar to being a food server, your income is cash. In our business not so much in tips, but definitely *cash*. Most food servers make much more than they report, and the same goes for HDVs. So, I am going to give you real numbers. HDVs incomes are relative. Relative to where they work, how often they work and their individual skills. Because I talk to vendors daily, and because I am a vendor, I can offer you an accurate average. Full time vendors working lunch shifts are averaging $50,000 annually. Some are making less and some are making more. I know vendors making well over $100,000 a year from one cart. But, to make this easier, you know your ability, your drive, and your personality. You know if you are happy with the spot making $200 a day, or if $600 is more like it, and so you continue looking for that perfect spot.

Later, I will break down all the costs. But, for now, I am going to use the average cost and this includes all costs: the food, condiments, napkins, propane, ice, etc., etc., etc.

Thirty-two percent (32%) is a good rule of thumb. You may be higher or lower, but this will be the most accurate for our purposes. Let's say we offer two (2) hot dogs, chips and a soda for $5.00.

$5.00

<u>minus $1.60</u>

Your profit: $3.40 per meal deal.

I always try to find a place where I can do at least one hundred meals a day. This means that after all my expenses, my net would be $340 based on 100 meals. One hundred meals are great, but, after awhile, you may desire more. So, you find that spot that allows you to sell 200 meals a day. $680 is even better!

Let's see what this does for an annual income. Now, I am not one of those pie-in-the-sky guys here to blow smoke up your butt. You and I both know there will be days you can't work; inclement weather, a sick child, neighbor's cats having puppies, or you have an emergency fishing trip to attend. My numbers will reflect an average – not a hypothetical, superman, alternate perfect universe theory where you can work nine days a week and your only day off is the second Tuesday of each week.

Let's use twenty days a month as our average. If you live in a cold climate like Northern Michigan or Wisconsin, your work year may require many consecutive days, and then you may take the winter off. This would be 240 days a year at $340; heck, stop right there! To be on the conservative side, I'm going to use half the 240 days a year, which is 120 days. If you work 120 days at $340 a day ($3.40 profit for each meal), and you have an annual net income of over $40,000. Not bad, huh? What if you sold to 50 customers a day, for 240 days a year? Yep, same income $40,000. I was just making sure you hadn't fallen asleep.

Now, I can tell by the way you stare at these beautiful words, you are not a slacker – you are a go-getter. You are the one who always goes the extra mile, never satisfied with mediocrity or just getting by. So let's run it up a notch.

One good location, like the location I found the second week I started vending (sheltered, available year round), and although I only worked it 2 days a week, I certainly could have worked it another day without boring the customers with my delicious dogs. More on that later. Back to my point – one good location at 220 days a year (see, I just gave you an extra 20 days off), with $440 daily in net sales (remember: net sales is your take-home profit), is . . . over $96,000 a year.

220 days X $440 daily sales = $96,800 Net Annual Income

Some HDVs only work events and I have witnessed vendors making several thousand, and even over $10,000 per day at a good event. Your income is only limited by your will, your drive and your ability to find the perfect spot or spots. Yes, I am going to cover more of this later.

Holy Wow!

There are currently 1,000s of HDVs operating carts worldwide, and more starting every day. Oh, no! Lions, tigers and bears! Oh, my! Competition! What will I do? Calm the heck down, take a sip and keep reading. As aforementioned (what I said above), the examples are with your only serving 50 to 100 customers a day. You don't need everybody in your town, just 50 to 150 (OK, you go-getter! 300. Either way, I bet your town has more than 300 people.) My point is that in your town or area, how many convenience stores do you have? Yet, miraculously, they remain in business. You don't need everyone. This past summer I visited Denver, Colorado, on a cold and windy day in the middle of the week, and I walked by two carts on the strip, <u>on each block</u>. It was ridiculous and, somehow, these wonderful vendors manage to eek by on incomes that corporate employees would envy. Don't feel pressured to rush into this business, because you hear about others getting in. There is plenty of time. Take your time, do your due diligence and make good decisions.

Example: Ever notice when you buy a new car, no matter what it is, you will all of a sudden see and notice more of these on the road than ever before. It's psychological. It's called the *red car syndrome*, I think. OK, I don't know, but it sounds good. *Red Car Syndrome.* The little red pill available in pharmacies nationwide. Because you have found a new interest, it will appear as though everyone has this same idea.

A lady, I'll call her Dani (only because that's her name), called me in a panic.

"I just drove over to Sam's Club to get a membership and saw two hot dog vendors. What in the world? This market is going to be saturated before I even get my cart."

Really? Are you serious? That's what I'm thinking, but I understand. With her newly found interest and her cart on its way to her door as we spoke, she was noticing *red cars* – er – hot dog carts that she had never noticed before.

"But, Ben, I drive this road almost daily and they weren't there before! One even looks like one of your carts."

I knew the guy who was set up at the Home Depot and, although I didn't sell him his cart, I had spoken with him previously about some custom work. After a little searching through my old emails, I informed Dani that Larry had been at the Home Depot for over five years. She was astounded! All this time, she had never noticed him.

A little luck doesn't hurt, but it certainly isn't necessary. Hard work, dedication, determination and that go-getter attitude will outperform luck every day. If you are lucky, real lucky, play the lottery. But if you are like me, then let's get up and get something done.

This is easy, really. All you have to do is find a good location; work real hard and you can make an excellent income. OK, you caught me, I said, "Work real hard". Yup, this is work; it can be hard at times, frustrating and it can mean missing your favorite soap opera sometimes. Or, getting up early to cut onions and prep for the day, or getting home and having to clean four or five pans and the utensils. But, honestly, I don't know of anything you can do and make as much hourly as slinging dogs.

I didn't mention this before, but the average day for a HDV is only 4 or 5 hours. Some, like me, found a location that only required two hours and my take home was over $400; that's over $200 an hour. Yes, I did go to college, community college, and I worked, slaved and studied for a solid 5.2 weeks. I think I earned a total of one-half of a credit. College has nothing to do with it. I found a great location, I only worked it two days a week and I grossed almost $1,000 a week. A total of 4 hours a week! I'll explain more later.

In my examples above, I gave a figure of 220 days a year working, but this is only about four or five hours a day. In actuality, it's a half day of work, 220 times a year. Or, combined, it's 110 full work days.

This is the no-smoke zone. You do still have prep times and clean up, but this amounted to approximately another 2 hours a week for me. Essentially, you can figure an hour to an hour and a half for each workday for the behind the scenes labor.

Finally, what makes this such a great business? Well, if you take out the excellent income, cash money, the tips, the friends you meet, the ability to set your own schedule, the short work days, the short work weeks, the free time, the financial security and the free lunches . . . then nothing. If you took all of that away, it would simply suck. The beauty is that it all that stays and comes with the package. I can't think of or find anything with as many benefits (that's legal), such as slinging dogs.

With a hot dog cart, you are mobile, and you get to choose when and where you set up. If you find yourself in an unproductive location, the fix is easy – hook that sucker to your car and move to a new location. A restaurant, a convenience store or any brick and mortar business, must study demographics and then, after all their due diligence, they must cross their fingers and hope to high heaven that the location is right for them. With the hot dog business, it's much like the saying, "Even a blind squirrel will find a nut every now and then." You can find that right location. You might pick a slow spot once or twice, but eventually, you will find that good location, then two, then three, etc.

At this point, I have either talked you out of the business, or you are 99.9% sure this is for you. If you are the first, then I beg your forgiveness for tricking you into reading this far and I apologize for the corny, slapstick humor. However, if you are excited, if you are one of the 99.9%, then let's get started. We'll start with Chapter 1. It just feels right – it seems like the perfect place to start.

By the way, the final chapter? It's kind of boring and nobody ever reads the conclusion, so I beg your pardon for tricking you into reading it first. But don't you feel better now that it's out of the way?

Don't answer that.

Chapter 1

In the beginning, there was a big bang

BANG! It was the sound of our economy crashing. It was the sound of companies slamming the doors behind the laid off and unemployed. It was the sound of the gavel as the judge ordered the foreclosure sale; it was the sound of our knees hitting the cold floor as we sobbed in despair. For many of us, it felt as if it were the end. Yet, it is really the **beginning**. For those of us, however, weakened by the recent calamities that have befallen us, we are fighters, we are winners, and we will succeed or else die trying.

With multiple furniture stores, multiple homes and cars, in hock up to my ears without any reserves, and with no warning, the housing market started down. Our mountains, overbuilt with rental cabins (my main source for sales), stopped building and it dried up almost overnight. I quickly tried to hedge my bets by closing all but one store in less than 30 days, hoping for a miracle that this one brand new store and its $30,000 a month rent could survive. However, the writing was already on the wall, and I made it one whole month in this new store before my vendors, my media sources, the electric company and loan companies cut me off. Days later, my wife and five of our children moved into a two bedroom singlewide mobile home. No income and, what I thought, no hope.

I tried tire sales and car sales, but both industries were facing their own pains with this declining economy. I sold things just to keep the power on and to keep us fed.

Then, one day, I saw a story of a family in dire straits, which had purchased a hot dog cart. As a family, they started slinging dogs and, to make the proverbial long story short, had dug themselves out of a very big hole with their little hot dog cart.

I was inspired. I couldn't sleep, and I started figuring out how in the world I was going to come up with enough money to buy a hot dog cart. I sold everything that wasn't nailed down. I even borrowed a little from my mother in law and got my first cart.

No courses, no pre-approvals from the Health Department. Heck no! I ignorantly jumped right in. Got licensed and quickly found out that I couldn't even sell hot dogs in my city limits. The Communist powers that were in place years prior had created ordinances that prevented me from capitalizing on the some 12 million annual visitors to the Great Smoky Mountains. I was devastated. What in the hell was I going to do?

I set up my cart in front of the tire shop I had recently worked for which, fortunately, was located just outside the city limits. My first day we made less than $200 and, day two through four were very similar.

Still, this wasn't bad money, but it certainly wasn't what I had read about on the web. So I humbly bought my first of many courses. I read the pre-buying pitches, about how you can make ninety cents out of every dollar, and how I could make over a thousand a day. But when the course arrived, it didn't resemble any of the 'pitch' material. My first course was a hard copy course with accompanying CDs. Turns out, it was a recording about what to do, as well as an interview. Then they spent at least (from what I could tell), ten dollars to have the audio converted by one of those free software programs, to print. It were as if a two-year old had written it.

"You can push your hot dome card to the stove and set up and begin to rake real monday"

So . . . the paper version was useless garbage and incoherent at best.

My point? I did it backwards. I got a cart and then I got my learn on. This is the expensive way, and I assume that you are reading this book prior to buying a cart. I hope so. Or, at least, you have watched all my free videos and got this with your new cart. Right? Again, I hope so.

Either way, I am grateful you are reading this and I hope it saves you from making costly mistakes.

After getting my fifth course, I had learned more from my own mistakes. These course sellers where selling crap, in my opinion. They worked very hard at marketing but they put little effort in the actual course.

Note: It was about a year later when I finally found a good course that I was proud to recommend to my customers.

I think it was my fifth or sixth day slinging hot dogs, when a repeat customer asked me why I don't set up at the local factory. He explained that at the factory where he worked, the third shift had two options for lunch: the wheel of death (vending machines) or bring your own lunch. I called the plant, finally found the right person and got permission to set up. This was when I first saw some light at the end of the tunnel. The very first night I worked from 11PM to 1AM, two hours that allowed two separate lunch shifts. It was cold, but the money warmed me up. I kept stuffing my pockets with all those ones and fives, and by the end of the two-hour shift, I was warm and toasty.

I worked the factory two nights a week. The rest of the week, I was trying out new locations and within seven weeks, I had purchased two more carts and paid back my mother in law all from the profits from the first cart, and I managed to pay my bills, too.

Two days at the flea market made me another $1400 a week, and then one day a week I would deliver lunch bags to a private school. I was making great money and it was all cash.

I still made some big mistakes but, overall, I was taking a self-taught crash course.

No, not luck. This was pure and simple dedication and determination. I also had huge incentives. My children felt that they had to eat every single day, whether it was hot dogs or bologna sandwiches. It didn't matter. They demanded food, housing, electricity and clothes.

Spoiled little brats, I tell ya.

CHAPTER 3

Before you do anything . . . damn it.

Where is Chapter 2? Who are you, Dr. Perfect? I didn't think so. Chapter 2 was horrible. I fell asleep, drooled on its pages, it soaked through and now what you need to do is be grateful that it didn't ruin Chapter 3. It's my book, and I don't need a Chapter 2. Are you some kind of chapterist? Some kind of smarty pants, Mc.Chapter police?

Alright then . . .

You have decided this is the business for you and want to get started as fast as possible. Get that highlighter out now, because it's about to get some use.

1. ~~Get your state health~~
Skip that. I need to give you this little disclaimer first, because I can already see them wheels a spinning, your eyes just widened, and . . .

Most states only allow certain types of foods to be served from an open cart. These types of foods are called **Non Potentially Hazardous Foods** (foods with a very low risk of growing bacteria). This is why most carts in most states, only offer hot dogs, brats and sausages. All of which are precooked foods. Some sausages and brats can be purchased raw, but they would most likely be excluded from being served. So before you get all wild eyed and bushy tailed about serving fried turkey feet or boiled lizard lips, I had to forewarn you.

Where was I? Oh, yeah. Number . . .

1. <u>Get your state health codes</u>. Probably available online, but definitely the fine folks down at your local Health Department would be happy to help locate them. This will give you a basic idea of the foods you can serve, and what the State requires for your cart. Some states require four sinks, and some don't require any sinks. See what I mean? Before you go hunting for that first cart, you need to have an idea of what is a "must have" feature on your cart. You will also want to find out what foods are allowed on an open cart.

2. <u>Contact your City/County office</u>. This may be City Hall, the Business License Division or the Commerce Office. No matter what the name, you can call City Hall and ask the operator who you need to see about getting a business license or vendor permit. Ask if there are any restrictions on vending within the city limits. Ask if you can use public property, like the courthouse lawn. Ask if you can use private property in the city limits with the

owner's permission. These are all questions you need to ask, and Code Enforcement should know the answers. Some cities allow you to be on private property with permission, even if it's in town. Some cities allow you to be on any public grounds with a permit. Some cities only give three-day or ten-day permits for certain locations. If you already have a location in mind, then you don't need to ask those other questions, but you will want to find out about your chosen location.

3. Contact your local Health Department, because they represent the State; in fact, they are the State. They are your local state agency that inspects restaurants, etc., and when you get a Health Department license, you will have a state license and, in most states, it's good statewide. So if you are approved by the Bebop County Health Inspector, your license will be good in Top Hat County and throughout the state (in most states). You will want to ask them the cost of the license, how long it takes to be approved once you have the cart, is there a charge for the inspection, will they look at schematics of a cart that you like and let you know of anything that could possibly be an issue or that may need changed. Remember: be kind and humble. These inspectors are often already overwhelmed with work and they may be snippy or snide, and they may even try talking you out of getting into the vending business. Keep in mind that they are paid the same whether they have fifty or 250 inspections to do. You are at their mercy, but remember they have to answer to their superiors. If you run into a problem, you can escalate your concerns. Your tax dollars and your

fees pay their salaries; ultimately, they must answer to you.

Note: See section AbCdE in this chapter for important tips and common errors by the HD (that's the Health Department).

4. Begin looking for a cart, but don't rush it. Here is where you will spend the most money, and you want to spend it wisely. After you have a good idea about what features are required on a cart, you can start your search. In Chapter 4, you will find extensive information about finding the right cart with tips for all situations, whether you are as broke as a convict is, or have some cash on hand. Don't skip over Chapter 4, so you can see the nude photos in Chapter 5. Those pictures will still be there, so don't skip ahead.

5. Begin making a list of potential commissary locations. In the HDV business, a commissary is the word given for the licensed commercial kitchen where you will store, prep and pre-cook your foods, and where the Health Department wants you to clean your pans after a busy day making money. See Chapter 5 for all your commissary tips and tricks, plus some insider secrets.

6. Call your State Department of Revenue; find out if you will be required to have a sales tax id. You may want, instead, to sit down with a certified and licensed accountant. He or she should be able to answer all your tax related questions regarding how you form your company. He or she will also be able to guide you as to whether or not you need a

Federal ID, also known as an EIN (basically a social security number for your business). Yes, I am going to cover this more in Chapter 6.

Some states will require you take a Food Handlers Course (see Chapter 13).

Section AbCdE

This is important, top secret information. So after you read it, tear this section out, cram it in your mouth and eat it. We cannot let this high-level secrety, classified, need to know only, information out. I know secrety is not a word. But it should be. If Sarah Palin can make up words, then so can I. Really, don't eat it. Maybe get a safe deposit box and stash this section away.

Contrary to popular opinion, the HD, under the guise of public safety and health, is only a government agency hell bent on making your life miserable. They will discourage your efforts to join the ranks of the many successful HDVs. They will go over your plans with a fine-toothed comb in hopes of finding a mistake so that they can use that fancy rubber stamp: FAILED.

I'm just teasing. Although there are some anal-retentive HD workers that are truly unfair and unreasonable, the majority are not. They are just like you and me; normal people, doing their jobs.

Note: If you haven't seen it, watch the movie *Food, Inc.* If this doesn't scare the shit out of you, then watch *Scary Movie 2*. Really, watch *Food, Inc.* – it will open your eyes.

The codes and rules that each state uses would create a gigantic book, thousands of pages with rules and codes that would make an attorney cringe. It's government bureaucracy at its finest. An HD inspector cannot and does not know every rule and code. Even if they do, which they don't, they will always have their own interpretation of those rules and codes.

Example: I use this example because it is horribly common; it's a battle I have fought for three years with inspectors in many states. A HDV will approach the HD, and the HD will tell the HDV that their cart must be NSF approved. The first problem with this rhetoric is that NSF doesn't approve carts or products. They only inspect and verify compliance to a set of standards. Typically, for carts, it's Standard 59.

I don't want to bore you to tears, but this is important. NSF, found at www.NSF.org is a private organization; they are not a government entity. They are the most known among the industry for certifying compliance to specific standards. Underwriters Labs is another one. You may be more familiar with U.L., and you have surely seen the U.L. mark on products before. U.L. is another organization that certifies compliance to Standard 59.

Some uninformed HD inspectors will state that their rules require all food equipment to be 'NSF approved.' Wrong! Wrong! Wrong! I have yet to see a state with a rule that says this. If you find one, you will have a good case for a lawsuit. Can you imagine the state rules or codes saying that you must purchase all your prescription drugs at CVS? Or, what if they told you that you could only shop at Kmart? Well, they don't; this would violate Federal Laws. What happens is, a zealous inspector will read, ". . . all food equipment must meet Standard 59 and/or be certified through an independent agency such as NSF."

Some states don't even require this at all. Only the areas where food is stored, prepared and cooked must be certified to Standard 59 in most states. They don't want you cooking hot dogs in an open dirt fire pit, but some states may only require you purchase commercial grade cooking utensils and materials, e.g. pans, lids and tongs.

What if your HD person tells you this? Simple. Ask to see the rule or code that specifically states this. If they pull it out, and you show them the error of their ways and they continue to be ignorant, then just call the State Director. All of these fine folks have a boss. Call the State Board of Health, or whatever it's called in your state, and talk directly to the Director or the Director's Assistant.

I found in one instance where a HD employee was telling this potential vendor the same thing. I called and spoke with her and she didn't admit her error. I called the State Director and he verified my position and called the county HD office. Still, this woman refused to reconsider her opinion. Later I found that she had family members with restaurants in the area and was simply trying to protect them from the evil HDV. I am told she no longer works with the HD.

Again, I am not trying to scare you. I want you to be educated as much as possible, so that in the event you face an ignorant HD employee with a chip on his or her shoulder, you will be well informed and prepared to take a stand.

Yes, you could just buy a NSF certified cart for about $1,000 more, but why would you? As I write this book, our carts are at NSF being inspected and tested. This process takes months and months, and thousands of dollars so I can understand why a manufacturer must charge more for a certified compliant cart. For those few who feel obligated to have that pretty NSF sticker on their carts, we at BensCarts decided to get all of our carts certified and will soon be offering that $1,000 sticker as well.

This isn't an option for most, like me, when you are starting out. Funds are limited or non-existent.

Huge Tip: When presenting yourself to a Health Department, do not make yourself out to be some ambitious, optimistic soul. Don't say things like, "Hey, I am going to have many carts! I'm going to put as many carts out on the streets as I can." These statements, even if accurate, are not the best approach. The smaller you appear, the less you are noticed. And, for the time being, you want to appear small.

Here is an example of what I would say: "Hello, I may be purchasing a small hot dog cart and we are planning on doing some catering and maybe work a few days a month." This makes you sound unimportant, and they will typically be much more lax with you. It's a great way to get your foot in the door. Remember, they are paid the same whether you are a vendor or not, whether you have one cart or ten carts. They are generally opposed to the additional work, so the smaller you appear, the more apt they are to help you.

Most new vendors don't face the dilemmas I have mentioned above, so don't worry. But, now you are prepared.

I'm not done, so sit back down. It's not break time yet. Another requirement, as mentioned earlier, is most states require you have a commissary. If you present yourself to the HD like I mentioned above, and you add to the conversation that you will probably purchase your foods as needed (the morning of the day you plan on setting up), then the HD may waive your requirement to have a commissary. In Tennessee, we are required to have a commissary, but I have a customer who used my advice and her HD inspector told her that she didn't need one.

Even if you aren't as lucky as she was, your inspector will be less apt to check up on you if he or she feels that you will not be out there in a big way.

Usually you will only see the inspector once a year, if you have made yourself virtually invisible in the beginning, they may only call you and ask where you have been setting up and ask to come by for an annual inspection. I have heard of inspectors wanting updates on when and where you will set up. By making yourself small and seemingly unimportant at first, you will likely avoid any such demands.

Once you have a license, it doesn't matter if you work nine days a week or twice a year. It's the same license either way.

I hope all that makes sense. I think that about covers the super secrety information regarding the Health Department.

CHAPTER 4

Let's find a cart

At first, I am going to assume that you have a little money stashed away. I will then cover some great ideas for you if you are as broke as a convict.

You have an idea now, on what features you need on a cart. One sink? Two sinks? Right? You did your homework, contacted the state HD and you are armed to make a good decision? Good. You're probably thinking, "I've got it from here; I already found several cart manufacturers online and I'm ready to find the best deal." Well, hang on there, Speedy. Have you even considered the possibility that you may get out there with your brand new cart and not like this business? It happens. Now you have invested your hard-earned dollars into something that simply isn't your cup of tea.

The best way to start out is as cheaply as possible. There are some great used carts out on the market: some people have purchased a cart that won't pass inspection in their state, others have found that the business is much too hard, and that they actually had to get off the couch and work for it to be profitable. Others may have gotten an old job back or simply found something they like better. It's what makes the world go round – this isn't for everyone and I am grateful for this as I enjoy going to a steak house or a Chinese restaurant from time to time.

But, if you must. If you demand the most cart for the money and you want it new then, by all means, check out www.BensCarts.com and check out our wonderful lineup.

Used carts are more abundant in the winter months. I assume again, for obvious reasons, it's cold, there are less people walking around and the once thriving warm spots are now cold and desolate. I see carts from time to time that were never used. I once bought a really nice cart that had sat in a garage for over a year. Never used. It was covered in dust for $800.

Start with Ebay, but do a local search – you will want to see before you buy, and ignore those listings that are too far away. Buying a used cart sight unseen can be dangerous. My favorite place to find a great deal is www.craiglist.org, because you can search numerous ways. Always try different spellings: hot dog cart, hotdog cart, concession stand, etc. Remember: if you can't go and look at it, don't buy it. Don't fall for the all too common listing:

Hot Dog Cart Brand New Ready to Ship: My buyer fell through, it's already crated and sitting at the shipping terminal, simply pay me and I will forward it to you.

These are scams, EVERY TIME!

Also, search under the business listings section on Craigslist. Some 'listers' don't know where to list their cart, and it ends up in some arbitrary section that could only be found by a thorough search.

Also, search nearby cities on Craigslist. For those of you with Firefox (free web browser), you can type in www.crazedlist.org and do a Craigslist search over multiple states, or multiple cities, at the same time. This saves having to do individual searches.

Before heading out to see those carts you have found online, you will want to make sure the seller has the title or title paperwork; otherwise, you will have a cart for which you can't get a tag. Also take along a propane tank, just in case they don't have one or it's empty. You will always want to fire the cart up before making a purchase, making sure you can adjust the flame well, making sure all the burners are working properly.

Determine how many burners are on the cart. If a cart has one burner, this will limit you when cooking. Let's say you want to serve chili and hot dogs. With one burner, you can't boil one thing and try to warm the other. One burner is almost useless in this case. It's not a deal breaker, but it may mean you have to change your menu somewhat.

With the burners on, put in some pans if they have them, and add water so you don't scorch the pans. After about 20 minutes of running the burners, you will be able to check under the cart and carefully feel around to see how hot the water lines are, and how hot the cooler is. If the cooler is super hot, you can bet you will need a full time job to afford the ice it will consume. Check to see if running the burners causes too much heat build-up in other areas.

While you are under the cart, check for insulation between the burner box and the rest of the cart. Look for insulation around the cooler also. I once bought a cart with two coolers, brand new. It was my first cart ever. It was a great deal, but one of the coolers was simply a plastic washtub with some wall insulation glued up on it. There were blank spaces and areas where it wasn't insulated at all. The second cooler, the meat cooler as it was called, was a metal box. It had zero insulation. It wouldn't hold an ice cube for three minutes.

Still under the cart? Well, get back under there. Check to see if the water lines are in good shape, with no obvious damages. Look at the gas line also, to make sure it is secure and protected. Now turn on the water and see if the water trickles or flows. If it trickles, don't be alarmed, this is typical for a gravity fed system and it is no problem. Make sure the hot water works and is hot. It should be very hot within twenty minutes of starting the burners.

Check the interior of the cart to determine the materials used; is it steel, cardboard or plywood? Look for problem areas. If the cart has been used and driven up and down the roads, you should be able to tell. My first cart was on a steel frame, but the compartment that housed the gas tanks, including the floor of this compartment, was made of pressed wood panels. Like the thin flimsy wood floor companies use to make a base for a tile job. Once wet, this stuff comes apart. I figured this out one night in the mountains of East Tennessee coming from North Carolina in the pouring rain. My spare tank fell through the bottom of the cart, and sparked and clanked as it rolled behind me. I was scared to death that it was going to explode. Luckily, it didn't.

When I arrived at home, the breadbox doors where bowed in, because they were made from the same material, and had warped from the rain. They were painted to look like some kind of heavy-duty composite material, but they really were just soggy wet cardboard pieces.

If you can, take a spray bottle with you. Fill it with soapy water and before you light the burners, turn the propane tank on and the burners off. Spray the lines, the burners, the valves and the regulator and check for leaks. If there is a leak, it will bubble up with the soapy water.

Check out the suspension. Make sure the trailer has leaf springs and is not just a frame welded to an axle. Otherwise, you will end up beating the cart to death when you pull it. Carts are relatively light and are prone to bouncing around anyway, but if the underlying frame is not on a leaf spring system, it will hop and bang all over the place.

Check out the grey water tank (the waste tank), to make sure it is accessible and easily drained. You will want to verify the sizes of each tank; the fresh water and wastewater. From your due diligence work at the

HD or online, you will know what your state requires in sizes. Most states don't care about the size of the fresh water tank, but they want the waste tank to be at least 20% larger. So if you have a 5 gallon fresh water tank, you will want to verify that your waste tank is at least 6 gallons or larger.

From here, it's up to you. If you have found fixable problems, you can make the seller aware of them and use them as bargaining chips to get the best price. I am often asked if this or that is a good price. You will often find used carts for sale for nearly what a new one costs. I know a man in Arizona that lost his son in an accident, and was selling the hot dog cart he had purchased from me. He sold it for more than our new carts. How? Well, most people want immediate gratification, and they want it now. Yes, they could order a new one from me and have it within a few days, but his cart was there and they didn't have shipping expenses. I was impressed.

There are still great deals, but putting a value on a used cart can be difficult. It will always be worth what people are willing to pay. I see carts listed in Florida on Craigslist that are ten years old, and they sell for more than a new one. However, I have also seen carts on Craigslist for $350.

If you are patient, there are some incredible deals. Even if you have to give up some features that you want, and you saved your money, you can let that cart earn enough to pay for your next cart with all the bells and whistles.

But I'm broke! I couldn't afford even a great deal on a used cart. Don't be discouraged; there are ways around this, but they require more effort. Start by placing a free ad on Craigslist:

"Looking for a hot dog cart. I am new and would like to share usage of an existing cart, or possibly rent your cart. Even if you have a cart that is not used on certain days, I would love speak with you. Call Bob @ XXX-XXXX."

You might just get a call or an email. What you are trying to achieve is the ability to use their cart when they aren't using it. Maybe even run it a couple of hours a day on their normal schedule to provide some relief. You can make them feel more comfortable if you are bonded – this means that you are insured to fulfill your obligations. Many insurance companies will bond you, and I'm sure you have heard of the tag lines for contractors, "We are licensed and bonded."

A bond is issued to protect others in the event you don't fulfill your obligations to them. They are relatively inexpensive. A typical $10,000 bond may cost you only $50.00 a year. It means a little more to a potential provider than just saying, "Take my word for it." This way, they know if you burn their hot dog cart up or break the law and start making meth on the cart, or you run away with the cart, they are covered. Note: Meth is great and all, but it's illegal, so don't attempt to open a meth cart. Now, on the other hand, if pot is legalized, you may want to offer free sample puffs. This will gain you a captive hungry crowd.

I know a feller, that's what we call people sometimes here in Tennessee, or sometimes, 'ole boy' or 'ole head'; anyway, I know this ole head that was trying to get started in business with no money and he actually volunteered to work for free to help this cart owner out. Quickly, he was in like Flynn, and had earned this man's trust. I know that doesn't sound great, but it beats watching Oprah and eating chips all day, waiting on your quick pick numbers to hit on the lottery.

Whether you do something today or not, the days will pass, nevertheless, and where you are a few days or weeks from now is ultimately up to you.

No, it's not easy and I never said it was. I told you in the final chapter of this book just how hard it really is. Remember?

Where are you going to be in four weeks?

You may be handy, you may have tools and the knowledge to use them. Always a great combination. You may have a little money, but can't find a cart that suits your fancy for the dollars that you have. Well then, why don't you just build one? Many people do and I have seen some amazing carts that have been built by people just like you.

There are courses online that will walk you through every step of this journey. I know for a fact you can build a cart out of plywood and have sinks and a drop in cooler for about $800. It would be brand new and it would have the features you and your state require.

You probably wonder, then, why I don't make carts for about $800 and sell them for $1000? Well, when you build carts for a living, for resale, then you are obligated to meet certain regulations. These regulations may require special licensing or special components, all of which cost lots of money. A manufacturer must adhere to these rules for public safety, so we cannot use some of the materials and components that you are allowed to use. Manufacturers are held to a different standard.

If you decide to buy a course online that teaches you how to build a cart, be sure that it includes video, step-by-step instructions and a materials list with places to buy the items.

Last, but not least, email some manufacturers or check their websites. See if they have any used carts available. Sometimes we get a damaged one from the careless act of a freight company. It's worth checking and may save you some money.

I always try to list used carts on my blog at www.benscarts.blogspot.com; if there are no recent posts with used carts, this means I don't have any.

Features to look for:

Steel frame
Water system
Cold storage
Space for two 20 lb. propane tanks (most states
require you have two on a cart)
Commercial Cast Iron or Steel burners
Heavy-duty valves and controls for the burners

Steam table that will accommodate the pans you want
Leaf spring or other suspension
Bread box/Storage

42

CHAPTER 5

You pervert; there ain't no nude photos here!

It was a joke and I can see you're mad at me. You patiently read, took notes, doodled and even highlighted in Chapter 4; all with the expectation of some nudie pics. Well, I am sorry. My wife won't let me look at nudie pics and, if I can't, you can't either. Besides, this chapter is all about commissaries and ain't no nudie picture gonna help you get a commissary. OK, maybe it could, but let's stick to the tried and true methods.

As I stated in a previous chapter, a commissary is just a fancy Vietnamese word for "place to clean, prep, store and cook that is licensed by the state." You can see why everyone uses the Vietnamese word. :>)

Most states will require you have a commissary, and they will want you to get a commissary letter. For example, it will state that McDonalds has given Beanies Weenies permission to use their kitchen to prep, cook, store and clean. Simple . . . right?

McDonalds isn't going to give you that permission, so the trick is find a willing restaurant owner. This can be a small mom and pop style grill, a full-fledged restaurant or a bar. You may know someone that owns or manages one of these. If not, then you will need to put on your happy face and get a shirt on, maybe shoes, too, and go out searching.

It sounds overwhelming but it's really pretty easy. Some people try calling these places on the phone, but that's just wasted time. Someone can easily tell you 'no' over the phone, but when you are standing there looking all pathetic, it makes it hard.

My script:

Hello, Mr. or Mrs. Commercial Kitchen Owner, my name is Ben. My wife and I have recently purchased a small hot dog cart so that we can make a living, and the State of _________ requires that I have access to a commercial kitchen for food prep and storage. However, because we plan on buying our products from the supermarket as needed and we don't prep anything, you would probably never see us. Either way, the State requires that I find someone willing to give me permission to come in during your normal business hours, and clean my pans or prep foods. Will you consider signing this commissary agreement so that I can get to work?

You may get a few 'no's. But like anything worth doing, it takes some effort. You may want to offer them a little money each month for the ability to use their kitchen. A small mom and pop gas station grill or sandwich shop would welcome any extra money. I never start with an offer of money, though. A free commissary is much better than one for which you pay.

Some vendors have that little gleam in their eye, like me, they establish a commissary and then charge other vendors for its use. It's a great way to make extra money if you have the funds to get one established.

While we are on the topic, do you know that some states will let you have a commissary at home? Yes, they will. Some require only a three-bay sink, a fridge and freezer, a hand wash sink and a floor drain. I put one in a portable storage unit all for less than $1500. I made this back in a short time with rents to other vendors. I could have put it in a separate room in the house, but I was doing it out of state where there are many HDVs.

I have found there are many places that have commercial kitchens – places that you would never suspect. In most states, if a church has a kitchen, it's commercial. The local VFW or Masonic Lodge, even some of the small hotel/motel convention rooms, have a commercial kitchen. This now opens up doors you never thought existed. A non-profit organization, such as a church with a commercial kitchen would be amiss to deny you. They enjoy a tax-free status under charity and non-profit laws, so I would not hesitate to ask them. You can even make a small offering for its use. It's a win-win situation.

Bear in mind, you don't want to ever make a mess or leave that kitchen in a condition that is worse than when you found it. I would leave it in a way that they could not tell I had been there. They are making a sacrifice and somewhat of a risk by allowing you this privilege, so be on your best behavior. If they are busy, go home and come back later.

Contrary to the codes, some vendors do their dish washing at home. Although the HD frowns on this and specifically restricts it, it's still done. And even though some statistics show a higher incidence of food borne bacteria in a commercial kitchen, the state sees fit to demand you use it.

Some states require you dispose of the wastewater in an approved commissary drain, and this can be a pain; but, I have found that most car washes have drains that meet stricter EPA regulations and can accept this grey water. So, I will pull through a do-it-yourself car wash, open my waste valve and then spray my cart down with the jet sprayer. I must tell you to check with the HD to see if this is OK before using this method. It stands to reason, that if the drain can accept leaky, oily, road grime, grease, radiator fluid and such, then it surely will not hurt to put in some grey water.

The best result is if your inspector doesn't require you get a commissary. However, if you must, then search for a friendly commissary or open one yourself in your home or at a convenient location.

CHAPTER 6

Taxes and licensing – my favorite part of the business! Not!

I have written on this extensively in my blog, but to avoid being called a lazy something or another, I am not going to simply give the link to that specific blog. I am going to painstakingly wipe the blood from my fingers and my keyboard, and suffer through the agony of this glorious subject.

Disclaimer: I am not an accountant, I don't represent one, nor do I have any training that would lead anyone to believe that I hold any knowledge on the subject that may be considered advice in any way, shape or form. The IRS powers-that-be do not allow tax advice to be given by anyone other than the licensed, trained professionals. I could not agree more. So I am telling you now, this is not tax advice or legal advice. It is my opinion and experiences. I advise you to seek the aid of a CPA (Certified Public Accountant), for any and all tax questions and answers, entity set up, etc.

Every state has different requirements; some states charge tax on foods, others don't. I happen to live in a state that does. If you are going to sell/resell goods, then you may be required to get a sales tax license, aka Resale I.D.   They are free and only require a little bit of paperwork.   You can complete most of them online; just look up your State Department of Revenue.   The benefit is that this allows you to buy your products tax exempt.   So let's say you go to Costco and buy a pack of weenies, for $5.00; you will pay just $5.00.

To make this easy, I am going to pretend your tax rate is 10%. If you decide to sell a hot dog for $2.00, you would need to collect $2.20 from the customer. Most vendors (to avoid the headache), simply sell the dog for $1.82 and add the 10% sales tax; this comes to $2.00.   So all the customer knows is the hot dog is two bucks... period. Simple.

Depending on the type of entity you set up will also play a part in what tax licenses you need.   For example, if you set up as a corporate entity, like an Inc. or an LLC, you will probably be required to obtain a FED I.D.   This is just a social security number for your business.   It's a way for the IRS to track your reporting.

Many brand new vendors set up as a Sole Proprietor; this simply means you are not a legal corporation. You are an individual with a business. For example: John Doe is doing business as *Doe's Dogs*. This is the least expensive way to start, but it has its drawbacks when it comes to what exemptions you can claim.   A corporate identity can claim many expenses that an individual cannot. The nice part is that you can start off as a sole proprietor and convert the company into a Corporate Identity after the money starts rolling in.

Corporate identities typically have more fees to get licensed; corporate filings, etc. You know . . . all the stuff an accountant does.

My uneducated opinion is to start off small, as a Sole Proprietor. You will need to get a business license from the City and maybe the County, also. You may be advised to get a State Sales Tax ID (resale license).

Note:

1. When you purchase items for resale and use your tax exempt (resale ID), the state has a record.

2. If you do not use your resale ID and you pay tax on the goods you buy, the state has no record of your purchase.

Words of Wisdom: This is a bonus, there is no extra charge, so do not send me any money. I'm serious, I won't have it.

OK . . . if you insist.

A good accountant can and will alleviate much of your income tax owed. This is OK; they are the professionals. You are saying, "Duh!" Right? Well, wrong. Out of any tax you pay, FICA taxes are super important. This is the tax that goes to Social Security. I know, probably by the time you are eligible, the system will be bankrupt. Well, that is not my point.

If while working one day, you hurt your back bending over to pick up that $20 that fell out of your pocket, and you have damaged it extensively, and you are no longer able to work. If you don't have private disability insurance, you will eventually have to contact the Social Security Administration to apply for disability.

Still with me? OK.

If you have paid in FICA taxes at least twenty of the last forty periods, you will, most likely, be approved. FYI: A period is three months. Even if your payments were not during the most recent periods, you will be eligible for SSD (Social Security Disability). If, however, you have not paid in at least twenty of the last forty periods, no matter if you paid in 100 periods prior, you get nothing. FICA is like a forced disability policy; fortunately, our lawmakers have created loopholes that allow us to avoid paying. This also allows the government to avoid paying you if you become disabled.

Example: If you pay your car insurance this month, and have a wreck this month, you are covered. But if you don't pay next month and have a wreck next month you are uninsured; this is similar to how FICA works, but the government does allow you to benefit from payments up to forty periods prior.

My advice: pay your FICA taxes every year.

Again, the above information is not legal or tax advice. Please contact someone licensed to advise you on your responsibilities as a business owner.

CHAPTER 7

Cart Features

You know what features you *must* have on a cart; but, what about the features that you *want* to have? Remember Chapter 3? I told you about non potentially hazardous foods? Sure you do; I bet you highlighted that section. You make me so proud. Proud to be an American, proud to know I'm free, proud to have known those vendors who - sold their dogs to me (to be sung to the tune of Lee Greenwood's *Proud to be an American*).

Say "No" to drugs! I'm teasing, I think it's just too late, I have been writing for hours and I type one line that has me singing with ole head Lee G.

You didn't spend thousands on this course to have me wasting your time with nonsense did you?

In most states, you can only serve non potentially hazardous foods, and you will want to make sure the features you want to add will serve you well. There is no reason to have a deep fryer if your state doesn't allow you to deep-fry anything. Most of us want all the fancy features on a cart; griddles, grills, popcorn machines, deep fryers and such, but the reality is that most states won't allow it. The one thing I have found that makes a cart stand out and it draws people like flies – **_a grill!_** Any griddle or a grill snaps and pops as it cooks; it sends off smoke signals notifying anyone within sight to come hither. It creates smells that are irresistible. At that same flea market I shared with you earlier, I was made to move my cart away from the building to another section because the smell of my grilled onions were sneaking inside, grabbing the people by the noses and leading them away from the inside vendors. They complained and after the first week, they asked me to move my cart.

If your state allows a grill or griddle, then I suggest you get a cart with one. You can even add one later if you can't afford one now, or if you found a used cart that doesn't have one.

About two years ago, we performed a test to see how a cart with a sink would do compared to a cart without one. I was of the mindset that it didn't matter. Why would a customer give a rat's ass? So, my best friend, Keith, bet me. We took two carts to an event that we had already booked, and we set up for about three hours. When the crowds left the entertainment arena and started flocking to vendors lining the street, the very first customer came to my cart; I knew it was in the bag. But, within minutes, a line had formed at both of our carts; Keith's line had noticeably more people. When the event ended, I had served seventy-one people, and Keith had served 206. Same carts, same menu, same prices and his cart with the sinks and water system did much better.

I can only speculate that a cart with sinks must appear cleaner to a customer, although I had a bucket of bleach water and kept my cart clean. There are a few states that don't require a water system and sinks on a cart. Tennessee is one of these.

I must admit, Keith's hypothesis that customers prefer a cart with sinks over one without, is valid.

Most states allow a cooler on a cart instead of a fridge. I still get requests for a fridge on a cart, but I want to tell you the honest truth; they suck.

The time it takes for an LP gas or a DC fridge to reach a compliant temperature can be as long as 24 hours. This would mean that you must keep that fridge plugged into a battery or to an LP tank 24 hours a day. If it's DC powered, you would need to constantly worry and struggle to keep the batteries charged. If you buy one that uses AC power, then you need to have an extension cord handy. This limits your ability to move, limits where you set up and presents a hazard to the pedestrians.

They also don't hold much food; most are 2.3 cubic feet and still require you to keep some coolers on hand. Most fridge units are not approved for commercial use; typically only the real large ones that you find in restaurants. If you choose to use one of these, your cart will be huge and cumbersome. They simply don't make sense. If you are required to get one, verify the inspector is correct. I have many carts in Washington State, but I have one customer that was told he must have a fridge on the cart. Instead of going over the inspector's head, he ordered a custom cart with an approved fridge that ended up costing him much more, contrary to my pleas.

Don't get me wrong, they do make some refrigerators that will function as you would like, but these are generally very expensive. A small apartment or dorm size fridge will work much better. However, they operate on AC power and, if on a cart, they must be used with a DC inverter, which is another expense. Not to mention the pain of keeping your batteries charged.

All in all, you will be much better off with a heavily insulated cooler. Coolers nowadays can keep ice for up to five days in 90º heat. It will be much more cost effective and efficient.

Many manufacturers use aluminum for the cart skins. This is no problem. BensCarts uses all stainless steel, but I don't think it really matters as long as the aluminum is thick enough to hold up to the occasional beat or bang. You will want to make sure the top is compliant, as this is considered to be a food service area and it will come in contact with food. But, in most areas, a plywood top cart with the right coating will pass inspection. Stainless is a hard metal and so doesn't need to be as thick as aluminum. Steel is graded in thickness by gauge. The higher the number, the thinner the metal. So don't be fooled. Pressing on the metal, whether aluminum or stainless, or even galvanized, will help you determine its strength.

Galvanized steel rusts quickly and is less dense; this means that it can deteriorate quicker than the other metals. But it's not a deal breaker.

Here's why: Let's say you spend $3,000 on a cart. If worked full time, this cart will potentially pay for itself 10 to 12 times annually. It may actually double that figure. Although you want a cart to last for years, if you buy a cart that the skin, the outer covering, was galvanized or some other lesser material and it began to deteriorate causing the cart to look bad, then you can have it re-skinned. It would then look brand new. If you had to buy a new cart every year for $5,000 and they were only made of pressboard, you still would have a money-making machine that pays for itself over and over.

I am not condoning cheap materials. I am not suggesting that manufacturers should build carts that don't last for years. I just want you to see the larger picture. The cart is a means to an end; it allows you to become independent, self-sufficient and secure.

Those that must finance a cart will often pay for that cart three or four times before it's paid off. This isn't ideal, but if it makes you enough money to pay your bills and enjoy life, even then it's worth it.

Note: BensCarts builds a tank of a cart. It should last you over ten years with constant use, and still it would only need some small maintenance-type items.

CHAPTER 8

Got a cart? Now what?

Now you need a place to put that cart, preferably not in your garage. You know what everyone says: *Location, Location, Location!*

This is the key to your success – probably the most important aspect of the business. I am going to share with you some excellent ideas on how to find the best location – one that allows you to make the most money in the shortest amount of time.

You will want to stop reading now if you are tired or it's real late at night. Wait until you have some quiet time and you are good and awake. There is a lot of info to cover and I want you to retain as much as possible, without having to re-read it.

The approach I use:

Hello, my name is Ben, my wife and I have a small hot dog cart that we use to make a living. We are going to be doing a small birthday party out this way next week, and wanted to know if you would like us to stop by and offer hot dogs to your customers. Our cart is fully licensed with the state Health Department and we are insured. It also requires no outside power or water. I think you will love it. Wait 'til you taste our chilidog or Coke and onion dog! We usually set up for at least 3 hours, but we'll gladly stay longer if you would like us to. We usually charge to set up, but since we will be out your way next _________ (insert the day) we would love to come for free.

Then just shut up. They will have to respond in one way or another. If they give some long excuse about corporate permission, I move on. You may have to try a few before one accepts.

Notice in my wording, I am not asking for permission; though I am presenting it as though I am doing them a favor. And, the truth be told, I am. It helps them by giving their customers a wonderful shopping experience.

Most of the time, they will want to know if you can come back. Some I have had to ask, "Hey, how would you like us to come back next Tuesday and Wednesday?

My first real set up was at the factory I told you about earlier. The human resources lady called me four days later and asked if I could come every night. She said the employees raved about the hot dogs.

That's when it gets exciting! You will end up with a customer asking if you can come do a party or some other event. I had a guy pay me to come to a tailgate party at a ball game. I had to remove my signs, but it didn't matter, because I was being paid a flat fee. One man paid me to come to a popular lake spot and feed everyone at a family reunion. You can see how quickly it will get so busy that you will want more carts. I was even called to come to a bass tournament and feed the fishermen and the small group of fans.

This business can really take off unexpectedly!

Now that you know what to say or how to approach someone for permission, we can focus on some great locations.

Most people immediately think a busy street corner with lots of pedestrians is the best or, at least it is what comes to mind first; and this is great, but sometimes you are limited by local ordinances that prevent this.

Factories: Especially factories that run 24 hours a day.

Hospitals: Excellent in my opinion. I know folks making incredible money at hospitals, usually working a late afternoon shift, when the cafeterias are closed.

Auto Malls: This is a string of dealerships all based in one centralized location; the employees alone can keep you in the cash.

Court Houses: Small town courthouses typically have one day a week, maybe two when they handle civil cases. Usually speeding tickets and minor offense hearings. They show up at 9:00 AM, and then they filter through the cases. They break for lunch and hundreds of hungry people file out to find the quickest lunch that doesn't require them giving up their parking space.

Business Parks: A group of businesses that are in a centralized location. The employees usually order the same take out or fast food every day. You can capitalize on their desire for something different and unique.

Flea Markets: Although some flea markets charge too much and have competing businesses that they own, these can be hugely profitable.

Discount stores: Dollar stores are a great place to set up, and I find that the first of each month is their busiest time. Why? Because many people who are on fixed incomes are bargain hunters; they have to stretch every dollar and they usually receive Government Aid Checks at the first of each month.

Salvage Yards: Busy, busy on Saturdays, and I know a guy who sets up in front of one of the national chains called *Pull A Part*; he rakes it in on the weekends. As more and more Americans search for ways to save money, the used car part industry is booming.

Note: Remember I told you about my city, and how they don't allow carts in the city limits? I find that by putting a cart at a salvage yard or an industrial park, or a similar out-of-the way location, no one is the wiser. I have never been asked to leave or even been questioned. I always get permission from the business or landowner first. I think the powers that be in my city just don't want you out on the sidewalk downtown, for whatever reason.

Public Boat Ramps: On a warm day, these are busy areas and can make you a hero among boating and fishing enthusiasts.

On a Lake: There are vendors currently vending from a pontoon boat out on lakes. This is brilliant but requires cutting through some major red tape to get going.

Landscaping Companies: A big retail outlet that sells trees, flowers and vegetable plants, see large numbers of customers in the spring and summer. Again, Saturdays are very busy.

Auto Parts Stores: Again, with the economy, many are doing their own repairs. Weekends are super busy at your local parts store.

Strip Malls: No, this is not an adult club; it's a group of retailers. Depending on the mall size, these can be excellent.

Clubs and Bars: Due to all the haters out there who like fresh, clean air to breath and have convinced our governments to ban smoking indoors where food is served, many bars and clubs now aren't allowed to sell you those healthy cheese fries or hamburgers, if they are going to allow smoking. Not every state, but many are like this. As an avid smoker, I am glad. The changes have given a HDV an excellent new source of income. Working a cart from 8:00 PM to about 2:00 AM a couple times a week could become a cash cow! I have customers that enjoy feeding these hungry club and bar patrons. One of my customers now has three carts she operates in front of bars, and she states her income per cart at over $1500 per week (she works 3 nights a week, Ladies' Night, and Friday and Saturday.)

Racetracks: Local dirt or paved tracks attract large crowds during racing season. Most already will have food vendors and most own their own food vending shacks. I was invited to come serve dogs at one of these tracks, because the owner had one vending booth and couldn't keep up with demand. Many of his customers would get upset and impatient waiting in lines to get a burger or hot dog. He had me set up on the other side of the raceway. He ended up buying a cart from me and now keeps his customers happy.

City Parks: With cutbacks in government, many city parks have closed their city-operated concessions, so this would be a great opportunity. I know someone that got a spot at his city pool.

Universities and College Campuses: If you have followed by Vlog or Blog, you know how profitable this can be. Even off campus where students frequent can make you a huge success.

Auctions: At Public and Private Auctions, the auction company will usually hire someone to provide food; this can be a great opportunity.

Multi-Family Yard Sales: I am sure you have gotten up early to go to a yard sale and found it to be lacking; either they are permanent yard sales or they have exaggerated the event to bring more people. Finding a true multi-family or church yard sale may require some effort and pre-screening, but I have been dragged kicking and screaming to a few by my wife and have seen huge turnouts.

I could literally go on and on, but from what I have mentioned above, you should have a good idea or two about where to get set up. If you follow my blog at www.benscarts.blogspot.com, I give updates on locations from time to time.

Events: Events can range from the County Fair, a big auto show, parades, fireworks displays, gun shows, electronics shows, concerts, etc. Really, anywhere large numbers of people are captive for some kind of entertainment. Vendors have made tens of thousands during events. Personally, I am not fond of huge crowds and loud noise, so I keep my distance. Fortunately, not everyone is of the same opinion, so when I do go to the County Fair, I'm in good shape; there are vendors and great food.

Event managers or organizers are online, and you can check with your city or county Chamber of Commerce or Event Director. The good news is, most event hosts carry an umbrella policy so even if you travel out of state, their license covers you to serve food and to operate as a business, however short lived. The drawback can be the fees or commissions that you will be required to pay, but if you are at the right event and the manager didn't allow too many vendors, then you will still fare rather well. I know of a man who took his cart to a concert and paid $4,000 to be there for two days, but he made well over $25,000.

Events can be hectic and they will require good planning and preparations. If you have one cart working an event, you may want to pre-warm the hot dogs ahead of time, transfer them to the event in food safe containers, and then heat them up on the cart. The more prepared you are, the faster you will be able to serve your customers and the more customers you will serve.

Your prices at events will usually be much higher. Not because you want to take advantage of someone, but because of the costs involved and the requirement to share profits with the organizer.

In addition to that, you also have more risk; you will have to purchase large quantities of food and drinks with no guarantee of your success. At a fireworks show, a friend of mine spent over $5,000 just in food to be able to sell. He was scared to death, what if it rained, what if he didn't do well? What if, what if . . .

I am not attempting to discourage you, but I want to give you enough information so that you can make an educated decision.

Lowes and Home Depot: Big Box stores are ideal; they typically serve many people daily. Both of these companies have contracted with Street Eats to manage their vendors. Also known as Streats.net, they provide Lowes and Home Depot with their corporate cafeteria also. The application process with Streats.net can be overwhelming – they ask questions such as: what you will serve, prices, your uniform, how much experience you have, they even state that they require two years in the food service industry.
All of these demands are obtainable. You can list, if you like, that you have worked at Bubba's BBQ and

Ribs, but they're closed now, just for an example. Honestly, they don't really check up on you. They have figured out a way to make money without having to do anything, and so they spend little effort actually doing anything. I have never heard of them inspecting a licensed vendor. I guess it's possible, but I really doubt that once you are paying them their monthly fees, that you will ever hear from them again.

They will hit you up with a rental fee, and the fee, contrary to what they say, is negotiable. They will want you to sign a contract that gives you no rights and them all the rights. It's not the end of the world, but I don't like companies that take advantage of people. In my opinion, they offer you nothing and you pay them for it.

I have some friends that work carts in front of the home improvement stores and they are very happy. In fact, one lady has worked at Home Depot selling hot dogs for fourteen years. See her video on my Youtube page. So if you can suffer through the red tape with Streats.net, then, I believe, it's a great location.

Walmart: If only we could all have carts at Walmart. Of all the big box stores, Walmart would have to win the award for best location to set up. Well, believe it or not, it can be done. It requires some effort and preparation, but is doable sometimes.

I have always taught that if you can associate yourself with a charitable organization, then you can help others and often make much more money. One of the benefits of an association with a charity is that you will be allowed in places that normally don't allow carts, even cities that don't allow them will bend over backwards to help you if you are a charity or associated with one (in most cases).

Getting associated with a charity is not that hard. For example, the Humane Society or local pet rescue center welcomes help and donations. If you offered 10% or so, you can usually have the benefit as operating with some of their (the charities) signs and shirts. One of my customers, Sabrina, from Indiana, used this method to obtain the only cart in her town, which, by the way, doesn't allow carts. She was featured on TV and newspapers and the mayor was ecstatic that she would help others.

The types of charity make no difference, but definitely choose one that is local; people love supporting their local charities. Some cart owners have obtained an actual 100% charitable cart or even formed a 501c3, which lists them as an official non-profit charity.

Well, how in the heck do they make money then? Glad you asked. Years ago, a famous news personality, Paul Harvey, did a show on the topic of charities. He broke down the numbers as far as, how much of their income/donations is used for infrastructure (running the charity, paying salaries, ads etc.) and how much actually goes directly to its cause. The numbers were shocking. Some charities have such a large network, that their costs are exorbitant with only a small portion used for good.

Note: In my opinion, charities should be required to be completely transparent. We should be able to access all of their records, anytime we like.

Do a little homework, if you get a chance, on how much the RED CROSS took in after 9/11 – you and I donated over one billion dollars. How much went to the victims? Not much at all.

Next time you decide to make a donation or text a donation, check which charity has the best records.

Sorry for my little rant, but it sickens me.

Back to the question. How do they make money as a non-profit? All non-profits have infrastructure, some more than others; nevertheless, they have costs and expenses. You, as a cart owner, even operating as *"All proceeds go to _________________,"* have costs and expenses. Some of these expenses are your food costs, insurance and supplies, and your own income. You still need to make a living right?

By helping a charity and offering *"all proceeds go to..."* you can still make a living. Let's say one day you bring in $1,000; your expenses and overhead are $325, plus your reasonable and fair charge for being there, of let's say $250, then you deliver the difference of $425 to the charity. It's a win-win. You get to help your community and make a great living.

Now back to Walmart. If you approach Walmart, you will most likely get a big fat "No". But, if you approach Walmart as a hot dog vendor raising money for the local __________, then you will stand a great chance. Remember, be honest and give back. I wouldn't wear out my welcome, though; one day or two a month at Walmart could make you a large extra income. You give 10%, 20% or more to a local charity and now you are a blessing to your community.

Recently, one of my customers called and told me he went directly to his Walmart to ask the store manager if he could offer hot dogs to the customers. No charity, no nothing. Walmart said yes!!! This Walmart does not have a fast food chain store inside, so I assume that's why they allowed it. He did share with me that he offered to serve their brand in condiments and hotdogs. This is the first time I have ever heard of Walmart allowing someone not affiliated with a charity to do this.

I have also had customers team up with whatever organization that was already going to be at Walmart, and assist them by giving them part of the days proceeds. One couple was able to go with the local volunteer fire department and, as they asked for donations, the HDV sold dogs, giving a portion of the profits directly to the fire department.   Win-win!

Start looking for your location now; and maybe even find two or three. I have worked three days at one location and then two days at another. This allows me to profit the most from each location's busiest days.

If you are working in front of Dollar General and have given the manager or some employees a free lunch a couple of times and built a relationship, you may be wise to ask what days are their busiest. These stores keep up with their own statistics and, with this info, you can schedule your appearance on those days. I was operating in front of a Dollar Store with a cart and found that two days a week were better than the other days. I quickly modified my schedule and found a location to work the other days.

This will allow you to capitalize on the highest traffic days for a particular location. Another benefit of a hot dog cart is the ability to pick up and travel to different locations easily.

CHAPTER 9

Catering and delivery

I have already given you some ideas for catering in the beginning of Chapter 8, but many vendors get involved in this business with the idea of catering only. They do birthday parties, office parties, holiday parties, grand openings, store closings, etc.

Regardless of whether you plan to cater, you will get asked. You are serving customers on your cart; some of these customers will be so impressed with your attitude or your theme and your menu, that they ask if you cater.

Catering benefits include having a set time for the job and usually a set price, which means you know what you are going to make before you begin. One hot dogger wrote me about his ten-year stint at a car dealership. He worked every Saturday for a flat rate of $600, his take home about $420. Not bad for one day of work.

You will get the occasional, "Can you do my little Johnny's birthday party?" Remember, it will take the same effort to set up and clean up after serving thirty hot dogs to some children, as it would if you served

400 dogs to an office party. I don't do the little parties and I have a minimum I charge. Your minimum may be different but, whatever it is, stick to it.

You can determine your minimum with a little simple math: figure what the minimum you are willing to do the job or event. Let's say it's $150. Remember, you will have set up and clean up, and you will probably only want to agree to one hour there for that fee. Divide the $150 by $5.00 (or whatever price you decide to charge for your meal). In this case, 150 ÷ 5 = 30.

Add it all up and there is your minimum. Costs per meal can vary depending on whether you are serving eight-year olds or eighteen-year-olds.

I use this method to calculate any catering:

I want to bring in the same as if I had sold 100 meals. My meal price is $5.00, and I give them a $1 discount ($4.00) and my minimum is $400. This covers up to 100 meals (two dogs, drink and chips). This guarantees you a $400 income, less your costs of about 32%. You actually profit about $280. Keep in mind, if they get a larger turn out than expected, let them know up front that you will prorate the additional meals at the same rate.

I am very fair when it comes to doing this. I don't count all the drinks they take, I don't worry about the guy who ate five hot dogs; I just simply serve food and let them have fun.

Let's say I bring 300 buns – that's 100 extra, and I know I will use approximately 200. When I finish the event/party, I will quickly count my buns. If I have eighty left, I don't worry about the extra twenty. But, if I have seventy left, I charge for ten extra meals. I essentially give them a fudge factor of twenty meals for those big eaters or that kid who drank twelve Mountain Dews. Most of the time, the person hiring you will overestimate the turnout; if they estimate 200 people, I will charge them $800. If they use less, I keep the difference. I don't verbally price it to them at $4.00 a meal. I base it on the number of potential people. In the example above, that is $4.00 per person.

Is that clear as mud now? Good.

Delivery: Most of us don't have time to deliver, but I have done it when the need arises. I have delivered thirty meals to a furniture store, and even fifty or sixty to a private school. If I am setup nearby, I will either call someone to come run my cart or have him or her deliver the meals. When I was setup on the side of the road, I dropped off flyers beforehand at a local private school, at a furniture store and some other places. I didn't say I would deliver, but the private school became a daily customer. They usually came and picked up the food, but I did deliver a couple of times. These flyers brought in business employees that worked nearby that would normally call in lunch from somewhere or would go into town and fight traffic for a quick lunch. I was convenient and had great food.

I know of people who run deliveries on a regular basis to big office complexes. They put the dogs in

Styrofoam containers and a brown bag, and deliver forty or fifty meals at a time. I've run hot dogs into the Courthouse when they would call me with a good order.

A huge worksite Foreman called me to see if, on Friday, I could deliver 200 and some odd meals to his job site. I told him it would be better if I showed up with the cart to cook and serve them there. He was excited when we rolled in and, since he was paying for everyone, I didn't have to collect money from each individual. I just smiled and cut up with the customers as they lined up. As you can tell I like to joke and kid around; I am not comedy club material, but I recommend you have fun with your customers. I will take my fake ketchup bottle and squirt it at someone or when I drop a hot dog; I will pick it up, put it back in the bun and ask what else they would like on it. You should see their faces. Then I pitch the whole thing in the trash and keep going!

One day at a job site (not the one above), but a similar situation where the company was providing free lunch, a big man was in line and I could hear him discussing how hungry he was and how he could eat the ass end out of an elephant he was so hungry. When the man in line before him got to the front, I announced that this was the last hot dog. I thought this man was going to blow his top, he started hollering, "Just my damn luck! I haven't eaten nothin' all day! I wait in this f'n line and now he runs out!"

I told him it wasn't my fault, that several people before him got five and six hot dogs – holy cow! He came unglued! People around him were laughing as I reached into the pan with my tongs and pulled out six or seven dogs at one time. I was laughing, too, and I quickly got his order done and, believe it or not, he threw some money in my tip jar.

The funner (new word: meaning more fun) you make it for them, the better the food tastes, the happier they are and the busier you will become.

I can find catering jobs easily by looking for the big yard sales, multifamily yard sales, church auctions, benefits and other events that are listed in the event section of my newspaper. I also look in the classifieds and on Craigslist for these one-of-a-kind opportunities. Simply call them up, tell them you have a hot dog cart and would be happy to come out and serve their guests. I offer 10% of my proceeds to them and then I charge my normal prices. They will announce to their guests, "Grab a hot dog from _________; a portion of the proceeds helps us. Win-win again!

Gotta love it!

CHAPTER 10

Deciding on a menu

I see HDVs go out and buy the cheapest products and supplies, no name sodas, no name chips, stale buns and cheap no name hot dogs. These vendors will need either to change locations frequently or close up eventually. No matter your prices, if the food sucks the word will spread.

I am not opposed to serving no name brands – well, at least I don't mind if the hot dogs or buns are no name. The trick is to sample different brands. Try as many as you like and find the best flavor to cost ratio. Now, if you are in an area where price doesn't matter, then by all means, buy Boars Head or one of the other premium brands.

Even before you have a cart, you can buy several brands and put different colored toothpicks in each one, cook them up and serve in bite size pieces or just test them yourself. The key is to have a blind taste test. Several private label generic brands are excellent.

In Tennessee, if you say that you're serving Vienna, which is one of my favorite brands, people will look at you like you're crazy! A popular food in the south is the little Vienna sausages that come in a can, but when people see your Vienna sign, at least in East Tennessee, they will think you're serving a larger version of that little mushy thing.

Don't scrimp on sodas and chips; buy name brands.

Chicago dogs are delicious, but try serving those in East TN or parts of North Carolina, and people will think you're serving a salad on a dog. New name: Salad Dog

Your area and the demographics for that area may play a large part in what you should serve. Many vendors up north serve Vienna, but go to New York and you will find more Nathan's vendors. Stay away from chicken pecker dogs! Wherever I have been, from out west to up north, people love all beef dogs. Hot dogs made from beaks and peckers are not going to win you any points.

Soft buns are also important. Don't go to the ten-day old bread store and get stale, old bread. You can be thrifty, but don't be cheap.

Anyway, always do some blind taste tests. I make sure my condiments are name brands; people love Heinz Ketchup, they love French's mustard and Kraft or Hellman's mayonnaise.

When you first start out and you're deciding on a menu, try to keep it simple. This will allow you to get familiar with your cart and serving in a rush. If you are offering five different dogs, sausages and brats, you will have more waste and more headaches. Maybe start with a normal hot dog and a brat or sausage. Your overhead will be less and you can always add as you gain experience.

In some areas, vegetarian hot dogs will do better than or as well as all beef dogs, so you will want to research your area and what others offer. Specialty dogs like Japanese hot dogs are a great idea, but you may want to make this in addition to normal everyday hot dogs.

Decide on something that will set your business apart. I know a man that offers around nine different types of mustard, and another offers multiple hot sauces. I use my Coke and onions. I also have a friend that serves grilled BBQ dogs.

If your area has a favorite soda, serve it along with your standard line up. Root beer is a popular one among many crowds, and I serve the bottled version for $2.00 each. A profit of $1.58 and I display them in an old washtub with lots of ice.

Use ice packs or gel packs instead of ice when possible. With your drinks, you can line the bottom of the cooler with ice packs and then add ice. Always use ice with your drinks. It's appealing, and I have set up at a location and sold three or four drinks over hot dogs. You'll only pay for the ice packs and gel packs once, and then you you'll refreeze them each evening; this will save you money and reduce your overhead. Water is important to serve also. Bottled water, even the generic labels, will do well. I keep those flavor packs on my cart, so people can add them to their water. Kool-Aid brand or Crystal Light are great.

When you get your first cart, have family and friends over for a practice run or two. This will familiarize you with the cart and how best to set it up.

When I got my first cart, I did a family get-together and incorporated my taste test at the same time, killing two birds with one stone.

This also includes where I buy my products, too!

- Hot dogs (all beef), Sam's Club, 8 to 1's. This means 8 dogs to a pound in a 10 pound box for a total of 80 dogs, for only $18.82, or $.24 each
- Buns (Sarah Lee), Sam's Club, 16 to a bag at $1.77, or $.11 each
- Relish (Little Sister), Sam's Club, 1 gallon at $4.46, or $.03 each serving
- Fresh Onions (50 lb. bag Sweet), Sam's Club $18.00, or $ .01 each serving
- Ketchup (Heinz,) 44oz. bottle, Sam's Club, $3.82 or $.02 each serving
- Mustard (French's), Sam's Club, 30 oz bottle, $.03 each serving
- Chips (Frito-lay Assorted), Sam's Club, 50 one oz. bags at $11.22, or $.22 each bag
- Candy Bars (assorted brands,) Sam's Club, $12.84, or $.43 each
- Drinks: Sam's Club is my faithful source, but I search the paper for the specials at the local grocery stores. Sometimes they run these without any limit, so I buy a lot. Sam's Club

average is about $.32 a can, but by buying all over, I get an average closer to $.28 a can.

- Napkins (Marathon), Sam's Club, 4500 for $18.77, or $.004 each. Less than ½ a penny.

- Foil Sheets (Bakery & Chefs), 500 for $11.02, or $.02 each. I use foil sheets, because they aren't as messy and they look better than the wax paper sheets.

- I don't buy a lot of ice; the only thing I have in ice is my can drinks. My condiments and dogs are in a cooler with frozen jugs of water or ice packs. Less than 1/2 cent per serving

- Propane is a true cost, and I have averaged it out to about $.015 per serving. This may be a little high, but it's a good figure to use. (That's $1.5 cents per serving.)

You're probably noticing that the websites that say that you make about $.90 cent out of each dollar, are misleading. I saw one recently give costs when tempting you to buy their hot dog carts, and it stated that the average hot dog cost is $.11. Well, I am sure you could find a hot dog that cheap, but no one would want to eat it. It even stated that a meal costs the vendor $.65 cent with a drink and chips. This is not true at all.

Food service distributors like US Foodservice or Sysco can be great sources for some of your foods. Carefully compare prices. Sam's Club and/or Costco have some great deals and don't require a minimum purchase. Most big distributors won't deliver to a residence and the portions are so large that you would need large

refrigerated coolers. I buy onions sometimes from
Sysco, and when I do a big private party, I have
purchased the 100% Certified Black Angus Beef hot
dogs from them, too.

79

CHAPTER 11

Record keeping

I know it's boring, but it's important. A successful business will always have good records and, luckily, with the HDV business it's super easy.

Keep good records and keep your business funds separate from personal funds. I am not going to bore you to tears here but, if you will purchase a simple business ledger or even a plain old notebook, and write down your expenses, separating them into two categories: operation costs and goods purchased for resale. Supplies will be the necessities that you purchase that you don't resell, i.e. pens, coolers, condiment containers, pans, your cart, etc. You will want to keep another list for the goods you are reselling, food, napkins, drinks, and ice, etc. *I advise you sit down with an accountant or good bookkeeper; they can advise you of all the deductions that you will be able to claim, such as your car, mileage, and even some entertainment.*

Keeping your receipts is a must, and keeping good records will help you make more money. Less than three minutes a day and you can have good records.

Having another section in your ledger for sales each day is important, too. You can write down your sales when you get home each day, along with the sales tax collected. I explained how to figure taxes earlier. Whatever you do, don't go home and write down your sales as $450 and then add up the sales tax on top of the $450. This would cause you to pay taxes you didn't collect. You collected $450, not $450 plus tax. So back out the correct amount. If your tax rate is 10%, as ours is (actually 9.75%), then you will write down sales of approximately $409 and tax collected of $41.

To make life easier you can tally up the numbers each week.

Obviously, you will need to take out some money for yourself. It's my favorite part of bookkeeping; paying myself. Write the amount you pay yourself each week on this ledger list also.

A good bookkeeper or accountant can help you with this and they are not expensive. Then at the end of the year, you simply give them your records and they do their magic.

Please remember to go to www.BensCarts.com for updates on suppliers, supplier specials, software, news, new products and lists of where you can get the best deals on everything hot dog related.

If you are handy with a computer, you can make a simple Microsoft Excel form for all of it – Quickbooks or Quicken can manage it for you also.

Another benefit to keeping good records, is if you decide to sell your business at some point. The better your records, the more it will be worth. You will have demonstrable evidence of its success. I will cover selling your business a little later in the course.

CHAPTER 12

Insurance

Carrying insurance is not something you do when you can afford it. Do it NOW! If it means doing without some feature you want, or having to buy your products at the local grocery store before going out to work instead of buying in bulk, then by all means, do it.

It's crucial; it's necessary.

Contact a local agent; I use State Farm, but you can use whomever you like. There are two types of insurance:

LIABILITY: This covers your business in the event someone sues you because they got sick, or if a hot dog explodes in their face and mustard ruins that expensive shirt. If your cart catches on fire and sets a nearby car on fire, or if someone puts their hand down on your hot steam table and burns themselves – whatever the incident, you will want coverage. Liability insurance is not expensive; I have a two million dollar policy, it allows for coverage of one million per occurrence with a two million limit per year. It covers personal injury claims and personal property claims.

COMPREHENSIVE: This type of insurance covers your equipment, or if someone steals your cart, or they back into it; the list goes on. My insurance company joined these two types of coverage and I pay only about $600 annually.

I was pleasantly surprised when I added my second and third cart and the insurance didn't go up!

Go over your coverage options with your agent, and discuss all the potential risks. My policy covers the cart while I am traveling also, so if some moron without insurance rear-ends me at a traffic light, I am fully covered.

If you can't afford a policy, my advice is, don't start yet. It's that important. Although I have never made a claim or had any issues, I would not want to operate without it. Most companies have an easy payment plan so that you can get started with very little out of pocket expense. You can also discuss a bond with them; these aren't going to cover as much, but they may suffice in a jam.

As much as I hate these check for cash places, I would say, just this once, it may be wise to use one to get you enough money for insurance. You can pay them back and redeem your check after only a few days of vending.

CHAPTER 13

Food safety

Did you watch the movie *Food, Inc.* yet? Unlike fast food places and typical restaurants, you will be preparing, serving and handling food right out in front of your customer. *Cleanliness is next to profitableness!* Make sure to keep your cart clean at all times, because no one wants to buy a meal off a nasty cart. When I was in Louisiana recently, I spoke to several hot dog vendors. Most of them didn't keep a clean cart, and even their personal appearance was atrocious. A couple of them looked homeless. It didn't seem to affect their sales to the thousands of drunk tourists stumbling up and down the strip, but I wouldn't have eaten anything from off those carts.

Some states require you to pass a Food Handlers class before you are licensed. This is usually a one-day class and some companies offer a guarantee that you will pass. They will simply let you retake the course if you fail. Don't get scared, it's easy. It's mostly common sense with a few facts on food temps, bacteria growth and sanitization procedures. You will actually learn a lot.

Here are some practices that will help you:

Wipe down your cart as you go. The hot dogs will drip as you prepare them and, although it looks like water, it's super greasy; be sure to keep a bucket of bleach water and a couple of cloths next to your cart.

Keep condiment bottles and pans clean. If you pick up your ketchup bottle and it has dried ketchup around the tip, you will gross your customers out.

Use food gloves. They are cheap. Replace them after each time you handle money or have to pick something up that is not clean. I use one glove on one hand and then I don't have to change gloves constantly. I am careful to use my bare hand for money and the condiment bottles; however, to hold the buns, I use my gloved hand. I still change it frequently to avoid using a glove with chili or mustard on it.

Keep a small trashcan next to your cart for customers and for yourself. I have two; I keep one a few feet away for the customers, and a little one for me next to my feet.

When you have to restock from your cooler, wash your hands before beginning to serve again.

To prevent needing to open cans of chili or unwrap hot dogs, I prep everything in advance. I separate the hot dogs into bags of thirty; my chili is already mixed and in containers that are easy to open and pour into the hot pans. I have onions pre-bagged, so I can take one bag and dump the onions directly into my skillet or hot pan. This will keep you from having to open a new box of hot dogs or cut onions out on the cart, allowing you to keep your cart cleaner. It also will speed things up. When you are busy, you don't want to have to stop and pull out a box of eighty frozen dogs and try to separate them so you can boil thirty or forty at a time.

When someone orders a hot dog with mustard, and you accidentally put ketchup on it, or they say, *whoa, that's too much mustard,* I simply throw it away and start over quickly.

Know your food safe temps; below 41° and above 140° are uniformly accepted as the temps to prevent bacteria growth. You will be required to have a meat thermometer on the cart and to check your temps frequently. I bring frozen hot dogs and they remain frozen until I am ready to boil or steam them.

Keep your appearance clean; if you have a small cut or sore, keep it bandaged and use a glove all the time. Keep your fingernails short and clean, and if you have long hair, keep it pulled back and wear a hat or cap. No one wants a hairball hot dog.

You will learn more during the Food Handler class, but the above tips are worth repeating.

Most condiments are acidic enough to handle being set out. I still put mine in cool ice pans to keep them fresh. If you are going to use packets of condiments, I suggest keeping them in a cool area, not setting them out in the hot sun. Although they will not go bad easily, the flavor can change and they can smell bad even if they are still safe to eat. Mayonnaise is usually not allowed on a cart, but some states allow it if it's given to the customer in those little single serving packs. Keep these in the cooler or on ice, out of direct sunlight.

Pickles, jalapeños and sour kraut are prepared with vinegar, making them acidic, and they are usually considered potentially non-hazardous. I keep them covered and on ice also (I use ice packs and gel packs instead of ice on my condiment bar.)

I am often asked about leftovers. Check with your Health Department on what they allow. At most, I have some chili, a few dogs and buns left over. You could probably take the hot dogs, and refrigerate them overnight and then re-heat the next day. If you are serving a quality hot dog, this will change the texture and I don't like them. I throw away my extras, my sliced onions that are on the condiment bar, the cooked hot dogs, the opened buns and the chili. The most this has ever cost me is a three or four dollars.
Plus, I am too lazy to package them back up and store. It's much easier and quicker to toss it all. This reduces the time it takes to clean up and will reduce the chance of bacteria growth and potentially harming one of your customers.

I will give it away before throwing it away; if there are people close by when I am getting ready to close, I will make up the remaining dogs, wrap 'em and hand 'em out. This is great advertising.

If it looks ugly, nasty or bad to you, it will to your customer also. I watched a guy this summer serving hot dogs and he used a bun that was ripped on one end and a piece was missing. Nothing harmful and it definitely didn't change the taste, but it looks ugly and most people eat first with their eyes. Make it look good. If the buns are smashed, I don't serve 'em. I take them home and my family will eat them.

CHAPTER 14

Prep and setup

The following list will help you determine what you need to take with you when you head out to vend. You will add things as you gain experience and create your unique system, but, for now, a checklist will be handy to keep you from forgetting something important.

Supplies:

You don't have to buy all these items to get going; some are necessary, others will make your job easier and allow you to serve faster. When buying your food, if you can't afford to buy weeks of inventory at one time, don't. When I started, I didn't have the money to buy cascs of hot dogs. I went to the local grocery store every morning for the first few mornings and bought my daily supplies of dogs and buns.

Get enough hot dogs and buns for your first day, 200 of each. If you can't afford that many, buy 100. Even if you buy 100 and sell out, it won't be a bad day's work for the first day. Now, keep in mind, if your first time setting up is in front of a busy store or you expect more sales, then by all means buy more.

Keep it simple at first by limiting your menu to only hot dogs and a few condiments, this way you can get the feel of things first.

- Coke, Diet Coke or Pepsi products, water and root beer
- Chips, 1/2 oz. bags or 1 oz. bags
- Onions diced
- Relish
- Cheese, in the South we like Cheese Wiz (1% cheese, 99% wiz)
- Ketchup
- Mustard
- Mayo (maybe)
- Hot Sauce
- Jalapeños
- Beef Bouillon cubes (I'll explain this later)
- Cooking spray (use this to spray your chili pan and the perforated pan and it will make cleaning easier)
- 2 coolers, one for drinks and one for your food items. Some carts already have one.
- Napkins
- Foil sheets, wax paper sheets or Styrofoam hot dog boats
- Garbage can and some garbage bags
- Food service gloves
- Paper bags for carry out
- Plastic knives
- Serving utensils: tongs, ladles, spoons and a knife (I use 1 oz. ladle for chili)

- Meat thermometer and one for your cooler
- Ice packs or gel packs
- Ice (pick up on your way out)
- 3 pocket apron (details later)
- $100 in cash for change (Fives and ones are best)
- Small folding chair (I have never taken one to my locations; since there is no time to sit, a stool may be even better.)
- Radio
- Bleach (get a small bottle)
- Water (I carry with me 3 gallons to put in my pans)
- Water (one gallon bucket to add a capful of bleach for your sanitizing solution)
- 2 or 3 clean dish cloths to have in sanitizing solution
- Small foldout table (if your cart doesn't have enough room)
- Pot holders (I take two so that I can take the hot pans out when I'm done, they cool quicker this way)
- Your Menu Signs (you can hand write or print some off your computer)
- Marker
- Dry Erase board and Marker (They are handy for doing daily menus and specials.)
- Balloon kit from Walmart or Party supply store

That will definitely get you going; but, remember: start with the essentials at first.

You will have a good idea about what is required to run your cart when you do your test runs with family and friends. Every time you have to run inside to grab something else, would be a trip you'd have to make to a store when you are out there working. Sometimes, this is not an option, so make sure you plan ahead.

I have some videos online that will help you set your cart up, but here is a list of things to check before pulling your hot dog cart.

- Tires - make sure they have good tread and no tears, check the air pressure also
- Wheel bearings - most carts have a grease fitting, squirt some in every 6 months
- Hitch and Safety Chains - make sure they are in proper condition and you have the correct size trailer ball
- Water tank - make sure your water tank is full of water (I flush mine with sanitizing solution every couple of months)
- Waste tank - make sure it's empty and the valve is off
- 2 Propane tanks - make sure both tanks are full or have enough propane in them
- Soap Solution - spray on your gas lines with the gas turned on, do not turn on the burner knobs, just the tank valve, this puts gas in the lines and then spray your lines and check for leaks, if it bubbles you have a leak, tighten and check again
- Lights - check your trailer lights, stop and turn signals
- Do not travel with pans in your cart

CHAPTER 15

More than Basics!

I want to cover some of the basics with you.

Working in cold weather can be a challenge. When the temps are below freezing, you have to worry about water lines freezing and busting. It also is painfully miserable. On my YouTube channel you can find a video of one of my customers who works in bitterly cold weather, he packs a propane heater and he keeps on slinging dogs. A small torpedo heater will work wonders.

Some vendors use a pop up canopy. They are relatively inexpensive, and will shade you from the blazing sun, and protect you from those midday showers in the south.

A solar powered or battery operated fan will help when the flies are out. A cart with flies buzzing around is not very appealing. Some pop up canopies have roll up bug screens available.

Picking a name for your new business is a fun part. Once you decide on one, it makes your HDV business feel more official.

There are some very creative names out there: Doggy Style, King Weenie, Mustards Last Stand, Dick's Dogs, Tube Steaks, Chili Dogs; you name it and it probably exists. This doesn't necessarily stop you from using one you have heard. If it's not trademarked, it is typically fair game. I would never try to snake another name that is being used in my area or even a nearby area. This would be unfair and unkind.

Boiling dogs has a couple of problems: 1. if you boil them too long, the hot dogs will split and this is just ugly, unless you can pull it off as if they are rippers (deep fried dogs). There is a fix for this problem, but it requires years of experience and honing your skills as a professional. Wanna hear it? OK. Don't over boil them.

The second problem with boiling is that when you place the first few batches of hot dogs in the water, the water tends to sap out the flavors from the dogs. This is why the water changes colors and why they call it dirty water dogs. Well what if you were to super saturate the water with flavor first? Hmmmm. Maybe with a beef bouillon cube or a can of beer and a clove of garlic, it works and you will love it; best of all they will too.

Three-pocket aprons. Why not four or five? Well, because the more pockets you have, you have to have baby hands to get into them. One pocket for change, quarters only. Now, if all of your items are in $1.00

increments, then you won't even need quarters. So, in one pocket, $1s, then another pocket $5s, and in the last pocket, maybe $10s. If someone gives you a bill larger than a $10, put it in your back pocket and make change out of the apron. This way you never get the money mixed up and when you are in a hurry you can accidentally give someone a $20 that you had in your $5 pocket.

There are benefits for using prices that end in $.50. Like $4.50. When someone gives you a $5 to pay for that $4.50 meal, then they're likely to throw the change into your tip jar. I still prefer my prices in whole dollar amounts.

Speaking of tip jars, we really need to talk about these. I love 'em! It's free money, and if you are offering great food and making the experience enjoyable, many of your customers will tip you. I keep a tip jar right on top of the cart. I have seen some great tip jars over the years, so be creative with a sign on your tip jar.

True story! I have made over $1,000 in tips in just one month. I have made as little as $1 in a day and as much as $300.   Either way, it's FREE MONEY!

If you have a sense of humor, use it. Your attitude and personality is what they are tipping you for, or at least it seems that way. I

have worked my cart in a bad mood or very tired and, on these days, I get fewer tips! People love the atmosphere if it's fun and lively.

The most successful vendors are super friendly, run a clean cart, dress nicely and are fun to be around. Here are some things I do and say:

I remember you; we went to different schools together. Would you like to supersize that?

When asked what type of hot dogs I'm serving:

Oh, these are 100% all natural FDA approved Chicabeefpig.

I make sure to mumble on that last word, and it will make them nervous. Sometimes, they will ask you to repeat what you said. I repeat the Chicabeefpig, mumbling again. Then I tell them the truth.

You'll have to get the timing right and know who and who not to tease. There are some ladies who are skeptical from the get go, so I try to joke with them differently. If it is a thin woman, I will say, "Now, Ma'am, we have a daily limit, so after this one, that's it."

Or, "The usual? What? You haven't been here before? OK, it will be our little secret."

I have stepped on some toes before or been taken wrong; I didn't make them mad, but I can tell they're thinking too much, and I will recover quickly with, "OK, I was just teasing with you and I'm sorry, so this will be on the house."

"But I already paid you!"

"OK. Next time, on the house."

I did have a very uppity up woman get an order, and I joked around a little like above; she turned around and gave me the finger. I immediately said, "Ma'am, I am so sorry. I had told these people that no way, you didn't look mean – you are really a nice person."

You should have seen it! She looked at the folks in the line, they looked at her and she was noticeably embarrassed. That, however, was not my goal. The back story: she had already gotten a hot dog and was standing off to the side eating it. She called out for me and asks, "Are these all beef hot dogs?" (real snippy like).

I shook my head no and said, "No, ma'am. These are imported from Korea and they are 100% dog." Some folks laughed and that's when she shot me the bird.

When she left, she was still eating the hot dog.

Often, hungry men will grab one dog you have made and commence eating it while you are preparing the other hot dogs for them. One time, a man ate one whole dog while I prepared his other two. He says with his mouth full, "What's the damages (as in how much do I owe you?)" I looked up at him with a straight face and said $21.50. Oh, my god! I thought he was going to choke. I couldn't help it and started laughing as he tried to swallow that last bite.

I will say on a multi-dog order, "OK. That was three armadillo dogs and two possum dogs. Let's see. Your total is . . ." this will always get their attention; its funnier if someone in their party is already eating one.

I had an ole head in line one time; he apparently hadn't seen the prices on three sides of my cart, and he ordered one hot dog. I began to put on his fixin's, and he asks, "How much are these?"

I said, "Two bucks." He says, "My god son! That's too much!" I picked up his dog and took a huge bite out of it and said, "How 'bout a dollar?" He was flabbergasted. Then I threw it in the trash, fixed him a new one and told him it was on me. That man became a regular. His name is Mr. Fox, and he even brings a chair, sits by me and talks to folks.

I know, some of that is a little corny, but it works for me. If I were any funnier, I would be on tour, so give me a break.

Chapter 16

More than just a cart

I mentioned earlier that one of the ways you can grow your business is by having a commissary that you can rent to others. If you live in an area where there are many vendors, then this can make you great extra income. You can help other vendors solve one of the obstacles required to become a vendor and make money. Another win-win situation.

Leasing carts is a great way to make extra money, too. When you find a great location and have to make a great living, you have just established a successful business model that you were able to duplicate. If you were able to advertise this business for sale, my experience tells me you will be inundated with calls. Better yet, with the millions of our fellow citizens living in poverty conditions, jobless and hopeful, you may be the answer to a prayer.

If, instead of selling the business, what do you suppose would happen if you offered the business as a lease? Well, I'll tell you. You will be bombarded, overwhelmed and astounded at the response. Here is a sample ad you could post on Craigslist or a local paper:

Make $200 every day!

Run my hot dog cart, location, licenses and customers

Already in place. Start now. Call Ben at 865.446 0660

How in the heck can you make money by helping others? How are you going to make money if someone else is running your cart? Easy. You can charge $50.00, $75.00 or even $100 daily for this ready-made business. There are many ways to do this, but I will cover what I consider the best way.

Now that you have a list of names of people who are ready to run your cart, you need to have a system in place for weeding through this list, for determining the best candidate(s).

My system:

I inform the potential Lessee (the person wanting to rent/lease your cart and location, e.g. Your Business), that I am looking for someone dependable, someone dedicated and someone who is honest. I inform them that they will be required to get a bond (typically only about $50) listing me as the beneficiary (see Chapter 4 for more on bonds.) They will also need to read my food safety instructions and follow all terms of the agreement.

Some states require you take a food safety course, and then you will be able to train and advise your Lessee on proper food safety. If your state does not require this, I would still go online and download tips and instructions here:
http://www.fsis.usda.gov/factsheets/basics_for_hand ling_food_safely/index.asp

I will list the terms and conditions that I require, but you may want to add or delete some of these requirements. Always get legal advice to make sure your agreement meets any possible legal obligations. The following points and conditions will need to be outlined in any agreement that you form. Keep in mind, some of these may not apply to your situation.

- List the Lessor (you or your company) and the Lessee (the person leasing your stand and location).
- List the location of the stand and any obligations that you are under with the landowner. For example, he or she may not allow you to set up before 11:00 AM each day.

- They must agree to abide by the safe food handling instructions you give them.
- They must provide and maintain insurance or a bond listing you as the beneficiary or loss payee.
- They must be at the location at the agreed times and days.
- They must provide their own products, but they must be the products you use. You do not want them selling chicken pecker dogs after

you have a reputation of selling quality products (of course, if you are only leasing the cart and no location, then you may not care.)

- Menu prices can only be altered with your written permission.
- Additional product options must meet your approval.
- They must clean cart completely each day (provide instructions on how to do this.)
- They must clean all pans and prep their food each day (hands on instruction is best.)
- They must notify you if they are unable to show up. (If you are providing a location, you do not want them to ruin the relationship you established at that location.)
- They must have a way to tow the cart and provide, if required, an addendum on their auto policy to protect the cart from all accidents, theft or damage.
- They must keep up the area around the cart clean, and follow any instructions you have established with the location.
- Require a Non-Compete Agreement. Let's say they decide to get a cart one day and they want to take the location you have been offering them. A Non-Compete Agreement, in practice, prevents this. I have found that a better approach is to offer them a buy-out. They lease the cart for _____ days or weeks or months, then for $________, they can have the cart and location as their own. Remind them that they will still be required to go get the cart licensed, inspected, find a commissary etc. You can see

that this list can really be much longer depending on the particular situation.

At first, you may only want to lease them the location for a profit-sharing opportunity. I would still require bonding but, you would provide the food, the rules, and you will provide clean up and haul away on the cart each day. Essentially, they are an employee. However, to avoid the liabilities that come along with having an employee, you may be able to lease them the cart as a sub-contractor.

They will pick up the cart from you each day or you would have it on location for them, and they would have all the required menu items stocked. You will know approximately how much to leave them each day, since you will have already established the location and have somewhat of an idea about the inventory needed.

You could charge them nothing and then pay them $.50 to $1.00 for every meal they sell, or every dog they sell. You would only need to keep up with how many buns you gave them each day or dogs and then count how many are left at the end of the day when you come by to pick up the cart.

Yes, people can be dishonest and throw away buns or give away hot dogs, but you will know the very first time if you do your count each day. Then you can send them packing if found to be dishonest.

Another way to handle it is to provide a cart; no food, no drinks. You provide insurance (they still have to be bonded), licensing, food handling standards and nothing else. They find a location, provide their own menu items and prices; they truly are their own boss. You could easily rent a cart for $50 a day under these terms. Then there is no inventory or counting supplies, and they are responsible for their own success. I would still require an agreement of some sort, because you will want to make sure they return the cart each day, or week, depending on your requirements. You may require one week's payment in advance, for example. You may still provide a commissary or require them to store the cart with you when not in use. You can determine these things once you have found people desiring to lease your cart. If someone wants to rent the cart and prepay two weeks at a time, I would give them a discount. Example: two weeks, would be $700; however, I might reduce this to $500. I have even leased for as low as $150 weekly if they are paying one month in advance, and have met my requirements on insurance, etc.

The money from leasing can be huge. If you are renting an average of 20 days a month at $100 a day, that is $2,000 monthly. You could buy a new cart every thirty days (rental days). Imagine having ten carts working; let's assume you are only making $150 a week per cart – this would be $1500 weekly income.

There are so many ways to create a huge income – a hot dog cart empire, so to speak, and, at the same time, be helping your fellow man.

People often ask me if some of my lessees end up being my competition. Yes. I encourage it. My goal is not to keep someone down or subservient; I want them to succeed. Many people don't want to be their own boss, and they don't want the liability and responsibility that comes along with self employment. However, some will want to be in full control. Don't let this scare you! I love it! There will always be plenty of locations and plenty of hungry people, so I would never lose sleep over the ambitions of one of my lessees and neither should you.

Many people do not have the drive or ambition to cut through the all the red tape, and some do not want to do all the legwork required to get going. These people are excellent candidates for selling your business. No, not giving up hot dogs all together, but remember how you found a location and had a licensed cart working there. What if that location is bringing in $5,000 gross income per month? What if it is bringing in $100,000 annually? There are people who look for these types of businesses to operate. They want to walk in and be able to start making money immediately.

This is an opportunity for you to sell, and sell for a nice profit. Some businesses sell for five times and ten times annual revenues. I don't recommend trying to sell for this much, but, remember: if your selling price is too high, they can just duplicate what you have done. However, if you offer a fair price for a profitable business, then you both win.

A location with a licensed cart making $3,000 a month net (take home) income should be worth $36,000 at least. If you want to make a business of establishing carts in locations for resell, then I suggest you offer this type of location for $10K to $15K.

Location making $3,000 net income: $15,000

Cost of cart, licensing, your time: $ 4,000

Your Profit: $11,000

Do that once a month and you are making a six-figure income.

Obviously, if the location was hard to get, you secured a contract and it makes more, then sell for more. It is all relative to the business model you are selling.

The better you make the deal, the quicker you will sell the locations and the faster you make money.

There are people across America with fleets of hot dog carts. There is a man in New Orleans with many carts and he pays his employees hourly wages. I saw an ad once on Craigslist for a company offering $17.00/hr to run hot dog carts. That was in California.

I have a customer who purchases customized carts from me, and then he sells the carts with his logo' etc. He has a meat company make a special hot dog that is his own recipe. All of his vendors purchase his dogs, and he's created a beautiful business and has opened in Orlando, Las Vegas and Seattle.

All of these opportunities, and more, are waiting for you. They aren't a requirement for your success, but the market for growing your vending business is wide open.

CHAPTER 17

Pan set up

When I first started in the business, I was very confused on the pans, the types, the sizes, etc. It really sounded overwhelming. I am going to give you the hillbilly class on pans, and it will all make perfect sense once I'm done with this chapter.

Hot dog carts use steam pans. This is just a term, and it doesn't necessarily mean that you are going to be steaming anything. Nonetheless, all steam pans, also known as kitchen pans, share a simple sizing set up.

A steam table opening is 12" deep, 20" long. Pan depth can be 2 inches, 4 inches or 6 inches. You will find many hot dog cart manufacturers that sell carts that only hold 4" deep pans. This may limit you, so please do your homework.

A standard (full size pan) is 12" X 20" and whatever depth you chose. If you are steaming dogs, you

can put a full size spillage pan in the cart opening. A spillage pan is what you would use if you were going to steam items; it holds water and is about 6" deep. You would place two inches of water in the bottom, and then place the other pans in this one.

For example: if you were going to only steam, you could put a full size perforated pan inside the spillage pan. Now, the water below in the spillage pan will boil providing steam above in the perforated pan. This process will cook your hot dogs and steam your buns. You would have a 6" deep spillage pan and a 4" deep perforated pan.

Don't panic! Perforated pans come in two common sizes: ½ size and full size. If you were going to use a spillage pan and wanted half for steaming, and then use the other 1/2 for something else you can. You could choose to use the other half with two 1/4th size pans instead of one 1/2 size pan. 1/4th size pans are great for holding kraut and chili or even cheese sauce. They still sit in the hot water, but they keep the food from burning or scorching; they don't have holes. You can also use one ½ size perforated pan and one ½ size solid pan.

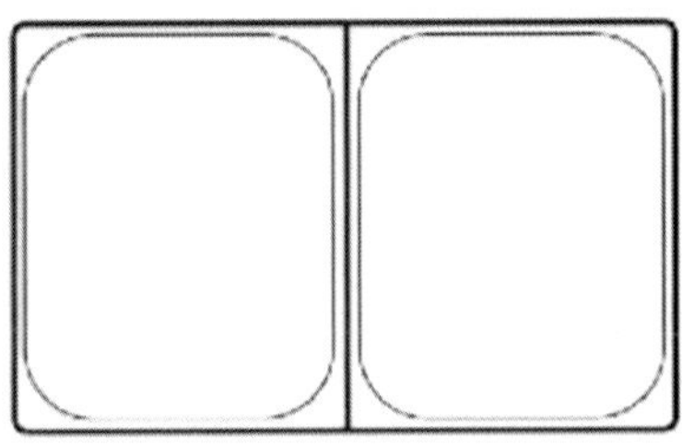

Remember what a full size pan is, right? OK. All of the other pan sizes are a division of the full size pan. This picture represents two ½-size pans. Removing the spillage pan and using solid pans make it a direct heat set up; I use this method for boiling hot dogs. I purchase a 1/3 size pan that is 6" deep, and I put water inside to boil the dogs.

Here's an example of using three  1/3 size pans: one for boiling, one for cooking onions and one for steaming. Yup, I said steaming. The trick is to find a 1/3 size pan that is perforated, and a 1/3 size spillage pan. It's almost impossible. So, they have invented these handy plates to go in the bottom of the pans, called false bottoms. They are slotted, and they allow you to put water in the bottom of the pan; steam comes through the false bottom, thereby turning an individual pan into a steam pan.

You can check out all the options and order different pans from many places. Here's one of my favorite companies: www.Katom.com

If you steam buns, I recommend a dome lid. These allow you to stack food higher and utilize more of the available space. You can imagine a standard 4" deep pan will not hold many buns if you want to put the lid on the pan, but if you get something like this, you will be able to cover an entire full size pan with a dome lid. Pan configuration underneath this doesn't matter, but this roll top allows you more vertical area to stack buns or dogs.

Pans used for food in the U.S. must be certified 'compliant' to food safety laws, and a hinged lid violates the codes of food safety, because bacteria can grow inside the small areas of the hinge. So, as of my writing, there aren't any Standard 59 compliant hinged lids.

If you have searched for a cart and found hinged pans, they will not meet state standards. The pan and lid may have an NSF or UL stamp, but once the cart manufacturer joins the two by welding a hinge, the compliancy is void. So be careful. I know a man that ordered a cart from a company, paid extra for the cart to be NSF, paid extra for the hinged lids, and when he was inspected in North Carolina, he immediately failed. All he had to do is go buy some new pans and lids, but what a waste of money.

Woooo Hoooo! You have it now! You know what a perforated pan is, a spillage pan and a one 1/3 size pan: you know how deep and all the other good stuff on pans. Right?

Okay. Please be careful when buying pans if the pans say 'stackable,' they are typically indented to allow for stacking. These types of pans, though, hinder you when insetting a pan into a spillage pan. You probably won't have any issues if you will always make sure the spillage pan is not listed as 'stackable.'

Chapter 18

Steam, boil or grill

From my travels, I have deduced that most HDVs steam their dogs. I am asked quite frequently about grilling dogs, and it's a great question. I think if you could ask 100 different vendors their opinion on grilling, boiling or steaming you would find that boiling is most preferred. I will expand on this to help you decide your method of attack.

Steaming: This is the process of using a spillage pan with the bottom filled with water. It holds the perforated pan that allows the boiling hot water below to steam the food.

Pros: Steam is attractive coming from a cart and it allows for quick cooking of frozen foods and steaming buns. Many of the long time doggers use this method with great success.

Cons: Steaming can change the color of the hot dogs. It also doesn't allow for long holding periods. Too much steam and your dog will shrivel and, some dogs, depending on the type of casing and meat, will split and turn grey.

Boiling: This method requires no explanation. Boil water, drop in hot dogs.

Pros: Quickly boil 30 or 40 dogs at a time. Turn off the heat when they're done and they can sit in hot water while awaiting their fates. *Tip: add a beef bouillon cube or a can of beer to the boiling water prior to cooking the first batch.* This will saturate the water with flavor and prevent the water from sapping out the flavor of the dogs. A garlic clove is a great addition also.

Cons: Often referred to as 'dirty water dogs,' it holds no negatives for me. I love to boil my dogs and find that I have less waste and great looking and tasting hot dogs, no matter the brand. However, dogs can split and bust if boiled too long. Six minutes from frozen to done is my rule, but practice on your cart to get the timing down.

Grilling: Grilling dogs is the most attractive and customer friendly way to serve dogs and involves cooking your dogs over an open flame.

Pros: They seem to taste better, and they are more appealing with grill marks. Grilling creates smoke from the drippings, which splashes the hot interior of the grill body, which creates an attractive smell and can bring folks a running.

Cons: Grilling frozen dogs is difficult, so you will have to open, thaw and stock more dogs. Grilled dogs don't hold long, so if you aren't serving them immediately, the skins get tough and start to shrivel. Grilling requires more space, since you can't stack hot dogs on a grill like you can when boiling or steaming.

You can either take a grill with you, or have it attached to your cart, which makes for great eye candy to customers. I know I just explained that boiling and steaming would be better, but if you are boiling and steaming, and then using the grill to create the aroma and ambiance, the customers love it. When customers start lining up, I often throw my soaking wet dogs from the boiling pan onto that super hot grill; steam and smoke rises and it smells so good!

Bottom line, I would use a grill, but only to touch up the hot dogs, not to cook and serve.

Sausages, Italians, brats or whatever, are great split lengthwise and then opened up and laid on top of the grill, this creates beautiful grill marks and adds to the delicious smells coming from your cart.

CHAPTER 19

Tips and secrets

I'm sure you have skipped to this chapter to get all the juicy info first. That's OK. It's your book and I can promise you I would do the same. I hope, for your sake, that you will still read everything and start off on the right foot.

I am very successful with the hot dog vending business and I know that you can be, too. To avoid costly mistakes and errors, I have left nothing out, at least nothing on purpose. I will continue to update my blog and website with new tips and tricks as I learn new things and better ways of profiting in the hot dog business. So please make sure you read and study everything I have to offer you. I want you to succeed in a big way.

Water Profits: Selling water on a cart is a must and will outsell sodas every time. I love to find new ways to profit from stuff I am already doing, and my water bottles helped me out. Most areas have a water bottling plant near them, and, even if you don't, selling water will still work.

Bottled water has a label, and this label can be changed; most bottlers will customize a label for you. No, I don't recommend putting your business logo on the label, but that's close.

Small businesses love personal ways to get their name out and to be locally branded. They spend lots of their hard-earned dollars advertising in the newspapers and local radio stations. I went to a local furniture store and told them that I was putting out about 1500 bottles a month. I showed them a label I had printed on my home computer with their logo and told them that I could have their message on every bottle I sell for a small fee. They gave me the details on what they wanted on the label and I ordered my water with that info. The furniture store even included a coupon on the label so that they could track the response they got. Smart. Because of the way this ad was delivered to a customer, it seemed to have a better response than the typical advertising.

I charge a flat fee. I figured up my cost of 1000 bottles of water with the personalized label and then added about $300 to this and that is what I charged the advertiser. The advertiser had a great ad that was more than a simple discount, but offered a free item with a mattress purchase. Boy, did it work!

I was now making over $300 a month from bottled water before I even sold the first bottle. Plus, the sale price of $1.00 was 100% profit!!!

You can do this with your napkins also, but it can be a little more expensive and time consuming.

If you can't find a local water bottling company, Sam's Club offers this service, but it costs more than the local bottlers.

Tip: When you approach the local bottler, tell them you are getting prices on 500 bottles with private labels, one ink color only and are comparing prices.

FREE HOT DOGS! "Impossible!" you say? Nope, it's pretty easy. If you have a local meat packaging and processing plant, you are already ahead of the game. A great way to find a local processor is to check your local grocery store, if they sell a brand that isn't a national brand, then, more than likely it is packaged locally.

You will want to go in person and let them know you have a hot dog cart and will be doing local events, and you'd like to know if they want to be your exclusive provider of hot dogs. If you have access to a computer and are skilled at any Photoshop-type programs, take a picture of your cart and superimpose their logos on the cart. This will help them visualize your set up.

On the side of the cart:

We proudly serve Bubba Dogs!

You may even consider sweetening the pot a little, and offering their ad for free on all your bottled water. However, don't offer that unless you must. Most of these companies never get an opportunity to advertise in such a personal way, and these types of advertising tactics are extremely effective.

Do your homework before making your presentation. The rewards can be huge, if you present it properly.

Tips:

- Create a presentation binder that you can leave with the decision maker after you make your pitch.

- Look up statistics on advertising to present, along with your presentation.

- Photoshop their logo all over your cart photos.

- Offer a one-year contract on a particular cart only. (I have multiple carts, and I didn't want to give up my right to sell other brands on those carts.)

If you do not have a local meat processor, you can always try contacting the big boys. From Oscar Mayer to Vienna, they all have programs. Nathans, Sabretts and Vienna all have vendor programs, but they often think they are doing you the favor. I would look at grocery store brands.

Onc customer of mine gets 60% off his hot dogs if he advertises that all of his dogs are provided by the local grocery store chain's private label. For example: stores such as Bi-lo, Winn Dixie, Food City and Publix may have a private label brand. I am sure you have seen these private label brands at grocery stores.

News: A recent customer called me to let me know he had a secured a location at his local Walmart. All he had to do is offer Walmart brand hot dogs and condiments. This Walmart did not have an inside food vendor, such as McDonalds, so he is kicking butt with endless customers. This was the first time I'd ever heard of getting a location at Walmart without being affiliated with a charity. I know I already told you this, but it's important and a great tip.

Now do the math! Free hot dogs and free water, could mean the difference of $300 in profit to $600 in profit.

I went to the local grocery store when I first started, and they gave me 10% off my business purchases. Not a huge discount, but, nonetheless, it helped me get going. Every dime saved is a dime earned. Always be mindful of ways to increase your profit margins.

Why not?

You are already set up, and the customers are in line. Why not offer some other items?

Best of all, these items don't have to meet any state food guidelines – they don't spoil, they don't have to be handled with gloves and they sell themselves.

Sunglasses, hats or any similar item will only add to your profits. I have sold 40 and 50 sunglasses in one day. Purchased for slightly less than a dollar and sold for $5.00, you can make a separate income from these

side items. The first month I made over $1500 on just my sunglasses and hats – profit!

Hats are excellent in some areas. I buy an assortment of hats and I hang the hats that have most appeal to the crowd I am serving. For example, downtown locations may do well with skater type hats. At the factory, I would carry an assortment of hats with sayings as mild as "I love fish'n" to "Cats: The other white meat." I even had hats with embroidered marijuana leaves on the brim and these sold like crazy. I did a catering job at a local church auction as mentioned in Chapter 8. I brought every hat I had with Christian sayings. In three hours, I sold every hat I owned. It blew my mind! This hat says, "Got Jesus?" and includes the fish symbol on the brim. All embroidered beautifully. These aren't crappy hats! They are quality and only cost about $2.50 each.

You can check out many websites, but I love <u>www.ctswholesalesunglasses.com</u>. They have hats and sunglasses. I clip the hats to my chip clips and let them sell themselves.

Tip: I always keep some Armed Services hats with me.

Note: hats that say Police or indicate law enforcement may not be legal in your state, so always double check before ordering those.

Belt buckles at a rodeo, purses at yard sales, and stuffed animals at flea markets and yard sale events, also do well. Don't go out and buy those items unless you're going to be doing a bunch of those type events, but the sunglasses and hats always do well.

Over time, I find that selling the hats at $7.00, or two for $10.00, does well. If you are at a flea market where others are offering hats, you may want to bring something different or drop the prices on your hats super low.

Anything over $2.50 is profit and it's all extra money anyway.

Tip: At Racetracks and Rodeos, the law enforcement hats do well.

I know a guy who sells his special mustard in small bottles and, although he buys his hot dogs from Sam's (just like me), he offers 6 packs (in zip lock bags) of his 'special hot dogs' for his customers to take home and cook. You have to admit the genius behind that.

His sign:

"Want a Barney's dog at your next cookout? Take home a 6 pack, frozen and ready to heat, all beef Barney Dogs!"

Find something that makes you different – something that makes you special. Offer several different types of mustard, offer gourmet ketchup or a special chili. You can offer the Coke and Onions I do, or a BBQ dog.

Special Recipe:

In one of your direct heat pans or in an iron skillet on your grill, cook up 3 sliced sweet onions. It will be a huge pile at first but as they cook, the onions reduce to only a fraction of the original size. Onions have natural sugars and they caramelize nicely when cooked down. I start with a very hot skillet and then add a little olive oil. Then I drop in the onions and add a little bit of Coke or Pepsi. As they cook, I keep adding the Coke until they are completely caramelized. It takes about 40 minutes for 3 raw onions to go from raw to ready. You can make road kill taste good with these babies – they are sticky, soft, slimy deliciousness!

If you're allowed, a special touch would be to squirt a little cream cheese on top.

Biker Jim, a popular vendor in Denver, Colorado, serves some wild game dogs that are made from elk and reindeer. The gamey taste is perfect with the delicious addition of Coca-Cola Onions and Cream Cheese. See it here: www.BikerJimsDogs.com

Jim delivers the final touch of cream cheese through a caulk gun and people are in awe.

I am not allowed to serve cream cheese so, every now and then, and purely accidental, a small chunk of  cream cheese will fall into my batch of finished onions and create a sweet creaminess to an already brilliant recipe.

I have a customer who offers a spiral cut hot dog that is an eye catcher, and the spiral cut turns what appears to be a seemingly uninteresting hot dog into a work of art. He even sells the little gizmo that cuts these hot dogs in little bags to his adoring fans. I have not tried these dogs but I spoke with a customer of his and they swear it's the best tasting hot dog ever.

In Tennessee, BBQ hot dogs are a favorite in the mountains. I take the already hot, hot dogs and place them on my grill. Then, using a BBQ brush, I coat them in a BBQ/bourbon glaze. All I can say is mmmmmmmm - good.

You've seen the meat injectors they sell. The look like an oversized syringe or needle, don't they? Some creative HDVs have made a special blend of seasonings, and they inject their dogs for an added punch. I have a customer in New Mexico that injects his dogs with a jalapeño concoction.

Get creative.

I keep an updated list of contacts and special offers from suppliers at www.BensCarts.com, so be sure to check there also, since I must update suppliers or special from time to time.

CHAPTER 20

Important contacts

I could really give you a list of tons of different contacts for supplies and stuff, but these are the ones that I have found that have the best deals and deliver in a timely manner. From accessories like tongs, pans, lids and equipment, like coffee urns and deep fryers:

www.Katom.com

www.Atlantafixture.com

www.akitchen.com

www.vendorsupplydepot.com

For ready-made signs, decals and stickers:

www.Ebay.com

For umbrellas:

www.Ewins.com

Organizations:

www.NAHDV.org
(National Association of Hot Dog Vendors)

Hot Dogs and other menu items:

www.Viennabeef.com
www.sabrett.com
www.nathansfamous.com

Food Service Providers:

www.usfoodservice.com
www.sysco.com
www.samsclub.com

Specialty foods (mini dogs, wild game dogs):

Tim MacCourtney (mini hot dogs)

Smoky Mountain Brands

828.736.3012

timmaccourtney@gmail.com

www.cowboyfreerangemeat.com

(elk hot dogs)

www.indianvalleymeats.com

(wild game dogs)

Costumes (dress up like ketchup, mustard bottle or even a hot dog):

www.amazon.com

(search hot dog costumes)

www.bigproductionsinc.com

www.balloonwarehouse.com

Your State Health Department Website:

http://www.nahdv.org/content/state-health-departments

Video tips, tricks and instructions:
http://www.youtube.com/BensCarts

My Blog with updates, news and helpful discussion:
www.BensCarts.blogspot.com

Online food handling safety course:
www.servsafe.com

For help setting up your company, corporation and licensing and accounting:

www.Legalzoom.com
www.quicken.com
www.quickbooks.com

Talk with other vendors, general help and advice:
www.facebook.com/Benscarts
www.roadfood.com
www.NAHDV.org

Chapter 21

Wouldn't you know it?

I get this book done, and BAM! I think of more things to tell you. Not random filler type information, but real money making helpful information. So, instead of trying to add some pages to the chapters where I missed something and possibly glue pages together, I am adding it here.

We covered events, but I really need to expand on this somewhat. I am not what you would call 'excited' about doing events, but they can mean huge money in a short amount of time.

After working events, I have felt like taking a week or ten off to recoup. An event can be overwhelming and you will have questions when you book your first one.

How much food will I need?
How many people do I need to help me?
How do I price my food?

Those are probably the most important questions you will ask yourself. First, because an event can be from a few hundred people to thousands, the answer is relative to the event you are doing. Is the event expected to bring 3,000 people and will there be 10 vendors or 100?

Don't panic. You will get the hang of it and, worst case, you don't bring enough food and you sell out quickly, thereby making a huge profit. How's that for bad news?

My advice is to find out from the event organizer what you can expect.

How many people will attend the event?
How many vendors selling food?
Other hot dog vendors?
Pricing: is the event host getting a portion of all sales,
and what pricing guidelines are available?

You've been to events where the food is outrageously expensive. Right? There are two possible reasons:

- they have you held captive and they know you're going to eat, or
- they are being charged a portion of sales, and they have to add to the cost.

It's usually both. So find out the averages, in addition to what the vendors are charging for burgers and other foods. This will help you determine the increase you must make in your prices.

Because of the variables at events (how many in attendance and how many vendors), it's hard to create a solid figure to give you.

Take the information you have collected from the event planner and do some math. If the event manager said that they expect 5,000 people and that you will be one of 100 vendors, then I would divide 5,000 by 100 to come up with 500. Expect to serve 500. That's nearly 1,000 hot dogs, and it can mean as many as 1,000 drinks, too. Usually, I sell many more drinks than hot dogs.

What if you sell out quickly and have no way of replenishing stock? Well, go home early and mark it down as successful, and now you have an idea on how to handle that event next year.

What if you only have 300 customers and you have all those frozen dogs left and drinks? Easy, they will keep, not 'til next year, but if you are actively working your cart you can use them over the following days or weeks. Three hundred customers is still considered a great day, and I bet you will consider it a success also.

Some events can charge huge fees upfront to the vendor. I have a friend that did an event, his first one ever, and it cost him $2,000 for the two- day permit. He was as nervous as a long tailed cat in a room full of rocking chairs! Fortunately, he could afford the upfront fee and gave it his all. The first day he sold out too fast, and the following day he was more prepared and he made several thousand dollars.

Selling dogs is one of those things that must be done through trial and error. You can be prepared as possible but with the variables, no one can give you the exact amount of product to take, or the exact number of people you will serve.

Start with some small events, such as a hometown celebration or school event, to get your experience. We all want to go and make a ton of money in one fell swoop, but it can be expensive preparing for an event. Take the basic costs for example, assuming a large event expecting 1,000 customers to your cart:

1000 drinks, minimum = $280.00 @ .28 a can
2000 hot dogs = $480.00 @ .24 a dog
Almost $800, and you still don't have buns, condiments, chips, ice, propane, extra coolers, etc.

Start slowly and work your way up to be able to handle the bigger events. You will be much more successful and less overwhelmed.

Help can be hard to find and, again, determining how much help you need is a challenge. Fixing hot dogs, taking money, stocking and re-stocking as you go, keeping the condiments full and drinks replenished can be overwhelming without good help. I have a great suggestion: FREE HELP! How in the world are you going to get free help? Do you know something damning about an in-law or a friend? I'm kidding.

Stop by the local high school and ask to speak with the economics teacher, or any teacher that instructs kids on entrepreneurship. All schools should have some kind of program or class that is geared toward business management or corporate studies. You know schools are always in need of funds, and if you offer to give $.50 cents from every meal, could they provide you with two students to help you for the day? You would be eternally grateful. They will fall over themselves to take this deal. After all, they get extra money, it helps students learn hands on, and you get free help while also helping your community.

Charitable organizations will often offer you volunteers for a portion of the proceeds, as well. Colleges and universities are a good place to hang a flyer requesting help in exchange for a contribution.

Can you believe I forgot to tell you all of that in Chapter 8? I have a mind like a steel trap; nothing gets in and nothing gets out.

I'm not done, so sit back down.

Cash is king, but some vendors accept credit cards. This used to be expensive to set up, but in today's wired world, it couldn't be easier. Now you can get a free device for your phone that swipes the customer's card, and then you have the customer sign right on your phone. It's easy and the money goes into your bank account.

The drawback is that there are always fees when accepting credit cards, but in a competitive market, you may need to add this expense as part of your costs to do business. You can count on about 3% of the sale to be taken out of your transaction for the fee from the processor. So if you ring up $1.00, you will get back about $.97 cents. Not bad, but it's still an expense.

Be aware of any other fees they might charge, such as a transaction fee. Some companies charge $.50 or $.75 cents to process the transaction. Too much, if you are making $5.00 transactions.

Here is a company that currently has a great program and it costs nothing to start. You will need a mobile phone that is considered a PDA, such as a Blackberry, iPhone or a Droid type phone. Make sure to get with a phone carrier that has good 3G or 4G service so that the transaction is processed quickly.

<u>www.squareup.com</u>

There are some other applications but, at the time I am writing this book, *SquareUp* is by far my favorite.

If you are working locations with professionals, like business parks and hospitals, I would have a way to accept credit cards. You will see better results, because many people don't carry cash anymore, simply due to the profusion of debit cards.

If you find a location that is profitable with many repeat customers, you might want to consider a 'loyalty card.' I know many vendors who use a business card that serves as a loyalty card. Buy nine, get one free. Using my previous numbers of $5.00 a meal, you take in $45 and give back $5.00. In reality, you profited on ten meals about $31 dollars; and, you have made a loyal customer. Who do you think this customer will suggest to the boss for the next company picnic or their child's birthday party?

These types of things build customer loyalty, which in turn, brands your business. I bought 500 baseball caps for $500 from www.superdiscountpromos.com and gave them away to my customers – the loyal ones. To this day, I still have customers wearing my caps.

www.nationalpen.com has discounted items from time to time, and you can take advantage of these, too. There are many websites offering these type things, and people love free stuff. I have given away pens, hats, key chains and other stuff, in an effort to build loyalty and to show my appreciation.

Dogs on a stick: I have a great customer who told me about how she serves hot dogs and sausages on a stick. No buns, just a dog. She barbecues the dogs and leaves some plain.

If you have a fun and creative idea that you are willing to share, let me know and I will add your story to my blog.

You're probably thinking that I have ADD by now, what with my final chapter all jumbled up with valuable information. Well, I think I have a good attent . . . oh, look! A squirrel!

When you are getting started, you will probably want to get a logo made. www.elance.com is a great place to find the right designer. You can get the work done for about $50.

Another trick I use is to keep my meats frozen at sub zero temperatures. My freezer will allow temps to minus 40°, and this will help your products in your cooler stay much colder for longer periods of time.

Need a hitch put on your vehicle? Check out www.Uhaul.com, because they do more than anyone in the United States, and they have better prices.

From here, the only thing between you and success is air and opportunity. You now have more knowledge than the average HDV. You have tips and secrets that only seasoned veterans have.

You have given yourself a huge head start.

But for you, the hot dog business may only be a means to an end – a way to create income while you search for something that you prefer. For some, this will open opportunities never before known and grow into a large operation.

I welcome your questions, your experiences and your successes, so please keep me updated on your progress.

As with anything, I learn daily and, as I learn new things, I will update my blog and website, so please feel free to check these often.

Keep in mind you will face challenges; some more than others, but now you are armed with good information enabling you to overcome any obstacles you might face as you get started.

Challenges? Yes.

But the rewards are huge.

With much love,

Ben

The Hot Dog Professor

Contact Ben:

Email: Ben@BensCarts.com